HIDDEN HISTORY *of* ROCKLAND & ST. GEORGE

HIDDEN HISTORY *of* ROCKLAND & ST. GEORGE

Jane Merrill

Published by The History Press
Charleston, SC
www.historypress.com

First published 2022

Manufactured in the United States

ISBN 9781467150484

Library of Congress Control Number: 2022935429

Notice: The information in this book is true and complete to the best of our knowledge. It is offered without guarantee on the part of the author or The History Press. The author and The History Press disclaim all liability in connection with the use of this book.

Contents

Acknowledgements

The greater part of the information in this book comes from authorities here in Rockland, St. George and the surrounding area—people who shared and made my research an unforgettable adventure. These include:

Doug Anderson, owner of Doug's Seafood Restaurant, Thomaston
Lenny Arey of Warren, Maine, autodidact
Larry Bailey, sculptor and St. George School Transportation Authority
Bill Batty, computer consultant
Eva Cushman, longtime villager of Port Clyde
Susan Devlin, president, Thomaston Historical Society
John Dillon, retired business executive and Spruce Head maple syrup maker
Mary Beth Dolan, curator, Jamie Wyeth collection
John M. Falla, president, St. George Historical Society
Marvon Hupper, artist and carpenter
Kevin Johnson, curator, Penobscot Marine Museum
Paul B. Keenan, administrator, Columbia University
Liz McLoyd, manager, the Strand
Paul "Gil" Merriam, retired history professor and author
Ann Morris, curator, Rockland Historical Society
Bert Witham, lobsterman

Preface

When I was living in France, I became interested in antique earrings. I drew them in sketchbooks. I had a good job, and I collected them. But later I lost the emerald, ruby, jade and diamond earrings, the ones of Russian gold champlevé, sapphires and Deco enamel. So I gave up. I had a ring made of a single French Empire diamond on black enamel. Then when I moved to Maine, in the winter months when the dark descended before four o'clock, cruising antique shops became a resort to keep up my spirits.

One day, a woman came into a secondhand shop in Rockland with various small items to sell. I saw sparkle and went over, and she showed me her baubles. "Those were Lucy Farnsworth's," she said, pointing to a pair of studs. "The museum is fixing up a historic house, and some of the jewelry has no value."

True, they didn't sparkle much, but a comparison came to my mind of Pierre Cardin's sales pitch of the Hope Diamond. They could indeed be very old cosmetic jewelry from the collection of a modest person.

The vivacious woman soon left when her husband came in to fetch her. She might well have embroidered a story to entice me, but what if the provenance of Lucy Farnsworth was true?

I bought the earrings for a few dollars. One had disappeared by the time I looked for them in my purse. The other joined my collection of "orphans." The incident remains my own, a quirky "hidden history" never to be unraveled.

PART I

ROCKLAND

Chapter 1

Introduction

A dynamic Rockland character, David Sulin, a U.S. Naval Academy graduate, has a smile for the world every day. Captain Sulin says he was paid for forty-seven years at sea to live his childhood dream. He quips that he has been to "180 or 200 countries, more than in the United Nations, and no place has come close to the warmth of this city. It was priceless to grow up here."

He recalled:

> *Life here as a kid was an adventure; you couldn't go where you were not known. And there were so many nationalities. In Rockland there were no strangers. There is no word in any language for how the spirit of that kind of community opens up life for you. My friends were Italians, Finns, Albanians, Greeks, Christian Poles and Jews. Kids were teammates and classmates, and certainly no one made fun of anybody's last name. Even now, when a contemporary and I look at an old school photograph, we may not recognize who the people are, but we'll say, "There's a Flanagan right there!" All our families were trying to get along, and they supported one another. When I delivered the papers, my mother told me not to collect the weekly seventy-five cents from a couple of the old ladies that I delivered to because she would pay me instead. People did for each other and were generous and decent. You met all economic and educational levels, and we kids were everywhere at once; we were like flies.*

Rockland. *Penobscot Marine Museum.*

Once a month, the Key Club at the high school had as part of their program a visit by members to a different house of worship each time. Usually there were two members of our sponsoring Rockland Kiwanis Club in attendance at our Key Club meetings. A regular attendee from the Kiwanis was the very well-respected Judge Allen Grossman. During the Key Club meeting, I would often suggest that we attend the synagogue for that month's church visit program. This was a popular choice with our group. Judge Grossman, a friend of my mother's, once asked, "Are you doing that just out of respect for me, Dave?" I told him, "No, Judge. We like the synagogue because all the good-looking girls are there." With a smile he responded, "I'm going to tell that to your mother!"

My mother was the first child in her family not born in Poland. Her dad was a stevedore working loading a ship in Searsport, and he was killed when a load of cargo fell and crushed him. My dad was born in Finland. He said that he was born in the sauna because that was the cleanest place on the farm. Because of the large Finnish population in the area during my youth and the sauna being a critical part of the Finns' social life, we sometimes "took sauna," as the old Finns would say, three times a week at different family saunas from West Rockport to St. George.

These sauna visits were social events where gossip and news were shared. When my dad built his new home in West Rockport, he built himself a beautiful sauna and held a regular Monday night sauna gathering right up until shortly before his death. "We Finns are a clean bunch," he used to say with a chuckle.

My mother was a nurse with a big heart and strong ideals. Although she did not work in the maternity ward, she was often there during deliveries at the old Knox County General Hospital and at the very least looked in on nearly all newborns and their mothers from the late 1930s until the 1960s. That connection to new life was something she cherished, and years later, she would see an adult somewhere and say things like, "He or she was one of my babies," or "He or she was a blue baby." She was very proud of being a nurse.

When I was six, my sister, six years older than I, went to a newly built school and had trouble writing because all the desks were right-handed and she was left-handed. My mother went to the superintendent of schools and asked where the left-handed desks were. He said they weren't in the budget and the need for them wasn't great. "We'll see about that," said my mother, and the next day, after she got out of work at the hospital at three, she got

President Roosevelt, Tillson's Wharf, 1941. He had kept his meeting off Labrador with Winston Churchill a secret, calling it a fishing trip. *Marshall Point Lighthouse Museum.*

Crescent Beach at Owls Head. *Rockland Historical Society.*

a clipboard and paper and went around the entire neighborhood covered by that school collecting names of children who were left-handed. The list was higher than the national average, but when she took it back to the superintendent, he still refused. She didn't budge: "Take it out of your salary," she said, so soon a truck pulled up in front of my sister's school with new left-handed desks….My mother always stood up for the underdog.

At twelve, I was working for Holmes Packing Company, loading cases of sardines into railroad freight cars. I was sent to the local Social Security office to get a Social Security card. The lady there, in turn, sent me to the superintendent of schools to get a permission letter from him because of my age. This was the same gentleman from the left-handed desk incident. He said he would write the note, but I had to prove that I wasn't going to quit school. "Mr. Kinney, you know my mother," I replied. He just grinned.

Her mother, my grandmother, came from Poland. She lost her husband five year[s] *after they got here. When she got her Social Security check, which had to have been small, she walked with it from her bungalow to our house, wearing an apron with big pockets, and I'd then go with her to the bank to cash it. Then we'd start the rounds. She paid her water bill, then her electrical bill; next was a stop to buy a few bags of hard candy to fill those large apron pockets and distribute to any kids that crossed her path; then came a stop at the state liquor store for a gallon jug of white port wine. We would now sit down and rest, and I would help her divide the remainder of her money into two piles. The next leg of our monthly journey took us to St. Bernard's Catholic Church for a visit with Father Goudreau and the nuns there. She would press one of the piles of her remaining money into Father Goudreau's hand with the words, "Give this to the poor people." Our final stop before heading home was, on alternate months, either the Salvation Army or the Red Cross, putting money "for the poor people" in their hands too. It was a long walk, from Pine Street in the north end to Main Street, across town to the Catholic church, downtown to the Salvation Army or Red Cross headquarters and then back home. She felt she was rich beyond all her dreams and was made happy by giving to others less well off than she felt she was.*

Above: Former Gregory farm, Rockport. *Nasser K.*

Right: Plaque outside the Nativity Lutheran Church, Rockport. *Nasser K.*

and Mary Ann. The elder Gregorys had eleven children in rapid succession, and Hanson was down the line. Like many Maine boys of the early nineteenth century, Hanson went to sea at thirteen. He was a crewman on a schooner transporting limestone. There was much to learn, and he had several promotions until he was accorded the honorific "captain."

When the Civil War broke out, three Gregory brothers—Jeremiah (age twenty-eight), Hanson (age thirty) and George (age thirty-two)—were registered for duty in the Civil War in absentia; they were off at sea. All the Gregory children lived their whole lives in Camden and Rockland except for Hanson, who was in Boston in his mid-sixties, while his wife and he went in different directions and she moved to be with her daughter and son-in-law in Brooklyn and then Montpelier, Vermont.

When Hanson went to sea, he would take a box of his mother's fried cakes. He wasn't one to carve scrimshaw, so once on the schooner the *Isaac Achorn*, he was "mawing doughnuts" and thinking about how the recipe could be improved.

Much later, Hanson recalled how he had poked holes in his mother's pastry balls in 1847 when he had been a teenager, transforming them to donuts. He had been off at sea and at the wheel of a ship during a storm, trying to eat at the same time. He realized he could stick one of his mother's cakes onto the spoke of the ship's wheel. When he was interviewed in the early 1900s, he said specifically that he had been eating the tough fried cakes he referred to as "greasy sinkers" when he used the round cover of the ship's tin pepper box to cut a hole in the middle. A tinsmith shipboard later fabricated a little device to make holes. The sailors called Hanson's donuts "life preservers."

It seems important to the story that while the earliest donuts were made of leavened (yeast) dough, after about 1840, baking soda was invented, and donuts could be made from non-yeast dough.

Hanson's technique was passed on to his mother. Mary Ann Gregory was cooking her treats when her fifteen-year-old son Hanson came home from the voyage where he was a mate and showed her the trick he had devised on the voyage: he could lighten up the pastries by putting holes in them. This way, her fried cakes wouldn't be soggy in the middle. He punched out the centers of a few uncooked rounds, doused them in the oil and voila! She was convinced. Mrs. Gregory was so excited that she sent him right back to Rockland with several plates of the fried rings to share with others.

Camden Library's archives have letters and other documents by which a cousin of Hanson Gregory's defended his cousin's donut origin story. A

Corner of Main and Park Streets. Sim's Lunch is at right, where the lobster roll was invented in 1927. *Rockland Historical Society.*

bronze plaque honoring Hanson Gregory is located in Glen Cove, Rockport. His birthplace is now the parsonage of the Nativity Lutheran Church, a spacious modern sanctuary that takes its name from the Gregory family's cattle barn.

Hanson Gregory's words stand as record because of that interview in 1916. At that time eighty-five, four years before his death, he lived in the Boston area at a home for old sailors in Quincy. Hanson recalled the hole he had punched in a donut as "the first hole ever seen by mortal eyes. Of course, a hole ain't so much, but it's the best part of the doughnut—you'd think so if you had ever tasted the doughnuts we used to eat." A March 6, 2002 *Washington Post* article titled "The Hole Story" gives some variants of the invention. I told Angelika this story, that Hanson lightened the cakes with a hole after six men fell overboard and sank to the bottom because of the heavy fried cakes they had eaten.

The origin of the lobster roll is more commercial. It involves a very popular Rockland citizen, Carl Simmons, who in his younger years made trips with his father to bring fresh lobster from Monhegan to Boston but preferred sales to fishing. Carl not only invented the lobster roll but also pioneered the small luncheonette during the Great Depression. The idea of a low-priced lobster salad roll came to him in 1927. He could keep the price at fifteen cents, since the lobsters came from his brother Harold Simmons, proprietor of Sims Lobster Pound of Spruce Head. Sim's Lunch opened on Park Street and, after a fire destroyed it in 1952, reopened at Park and Union Streets. The ten-cent jars of Cain's Mayonnaise were too small to meet the luncheonette's needs, so Carl asked Cain's for mayonnaise in gallon containers. At first, the people at Cain's laughed, but eventually they shipped his and other restaurants a "hotel size."

Chapter 4

Naming a Town

The year 1848 was a uniquely restless one. A social and cultural firestorm began in Europe with a revolution in France in February, and this engendered about fifty more revolutions in other countries independent of one another. Gold had been discovered at Sutter Creek, California, in January, and by December, President James Polk had validated the news and the gold rush was in full swing; 100,000 people who became known as the Forty-Niners arrived in California to prospect. The first women's rights convention occurred in Seneca Falls, New York, in July. The organizers, Lucretia Mott and Elizabeth Cady Stanton, had met at the World Anti-Slavery Convention in London in 1840. They were indignant at being barred from speaking at that gathering, and this experience helped propel them to launch the women's suffrage movement.

On the rocky, forested shores of Maine, the restlessness was evident in the separation of a new town from Thomaston. Thomaston was a proud town of Yankee sea captains, and now the area that would become Rockland was coming up in the world and felt a need for a separate government. A vote decided the citizens in favor of the separation, the state gave approval to the plan and East Thomaston was separated from the parent town. A town court and the incorporation of a bank rapidly followed. Twenty local young men joined the first wave of those who left the quiet scene of their home to seek their fortunes in the West. The first limekiln company was incorporated, and 125 dwellings were built. A new schoolhouse was finished in the middle of town on Grace Street, and after considerable

Rockland Courthouse. *Nasser K.*

discussion, the new educational model known as the Prussian system was adopted, dividing pupils into grades.

Since the separation from Thomaston occurred in early July 1848, the first Fourth of July celebration of the new town happened in 1849. It was a mostly restrained affair, drawing crowds locally and from the neighboring towns. Cyrus Eaton in his *History of Thomaston, Rockland, and South Thomaston, Maine* (1865) pointed out that the new town was intended to be a dry one, a haven of temperance. Meanwhile, further licenses to sell alcohol were granted, which led to a store being blown up. Hiram Berry was the parade marshal.

On the red-letter day, there were marchers, banners, an oration by a minister from Bath at Rankin's Orchard and a dinner by E.W. Pendleton

Quarry mining. *Rockland Historical Society.*

in "a special pavilion." However, a terrible event blighted the holiday and suggested that the protocol of future celebrations needed more working out. Writes Eaton, "One occurrence only, marred its pleasure. This was the premature discharge of a cannon by which the right arm of Robert Thomas was so badly mangled as to require amputation."

President Taft peering into the deepest lime quarry in the world from the Pleasant Street Bridge, 1910. *Rockland Historical Society.*

Main Street, Rockland, in winter. *Rockland Historical Society.*

Curiously, having relayed the tragic accident, this early historian of Rockland goes on to enumerate all sorts of other misfortunates in its wake—a captain's house consumed by fire, a workman losing his sight and one hand in a lime quarry and another captain tangling his foot in the line when dropping anchor in the harbor, being drawn overboard and drowning. On Sea Street, a carpenter in an old boat builder's shop died instantly when the weight of corn and flour stored on the floor above caused it to collapse. Always looking on the bright side when Rockland was concerned, Eaton's next and last paragraph of his entry on 1849 turns to the ever-present topic of weather: "The year began with fine sleighing and severe weather; the harbor February 22d being frozen over further than the eye could see. The week ending August 17th was most oppressive; the thermometer indicating between 95 and 103 degrees of heat, with an atmosphere of lime dust by day and fog by night." Despite his sprightly words, he was predicting an unfavorable aspect of a lucrative industry.

On the surface, the next chapter of the naming of the town seems whimsical. In May 1850, a vote was passed to change the name from East Thomaston to Rockland, and the selectmen were instructed to petition the state legislature, a petition granted by an act of July 17, 1850. A further official change was to the city of Rockland, one of the five cities of the state in 1854. Quarrying lime rock by now competed with shipbuilding, and steamers were replacing sailing vessels. Henceforth, Eaton explains, the lime would be known not as Thomaston lime but Rockland lime, a gratifying name change in his opinion, "when it is considered that its quarries of lime-rock are the foundation on which the prosperity of the place rests all must acknowledge to be an appropriate one."

Chapter 5

Mertie B. Crowley

Between 1896 and 1922, seventy-five five-masted schooners were built on the East and West Coasts of the United States. They were cargo ships to carry ice or coal long distances, as were ten tall ships built with six masts.

These were traditional fore-and-aft-rigged sailing schooners; however, their sails were raised and lowered by steam power. They were fast, held a vast amount of cargo and didn't require large crews. One of them, the *Mertie B. Crowley*, was built and launched from a Rockland shipyard on Atlantic Street in the South End of town at the east end of Mechanic Street by Cobb, Butler & Company (founded by Francis Cobb). Work began on it in October 1906, and it was launched in August 1907. The ship was 410 feet long from jibboom to spanker-boom tip, with six masts that rose 122 feet tall. The Rockland Military Band played as an estimated six thousand to ten thousand people witnessed the launching. A radio commentator on WBZ Boston, Alton Hall Blackington, would recall watching, as a boy of thirteen, Mrs. Mertie Crowley, elegant in a white serge suit and big hat with yellow plumes and roses, smash the bottle of champagne against the hull of her namesake. Blackington sold enough copies of the photo he had taken on his Brownie camera to pay for a new pair of shoes.

An important person in the throng must have been John J. Wardwell (born 1852), a master carpenter who designed the first six-master at the Holly M. Bean Yard in Camden. After the *George G. Wells* was launched, Wardwell moved to Rockland to continue building ships—eighty in all. He lived at the

Launch of the six-masted schooner *Mertie B. Crowley* from a Rockland shipyard, 1907. *Rockland Historical Society.*

corner of Fulton and Suffolk Streets in a fine house with beautiful sunburst carved wood detail at the angles of its three roofs.

Though it was expensive to maintain and operate, for three years the *Crowley* made the expected profits as a coal carrier. The ship was sailing from Newport News, Virginia, to Boston when it was blasted by a nor'easter and wrecked on the shoals of Edgartown in January 1910 in the Vineyard Sound. The captain was fourteen miles off course; he saw a beacon in the fog that he thought was Long Island light but was actually Block Island light. The Coast Guard and other rescue boats could not reach the ship during the night. Layers of ice shards pelted the slippery deck, and Captain Haskell and his wife, Ida, and thirteen crewmen climbed up the masts and lashed themselves onto the rigging of the sinking ship. The next morning, the *Crowley* had broken in half and its stern had sunk; the forward section and masts and riggings were all that remained. Captain Levi Jackson, a fearless five-foot-tall fisherman, and his crew from Martha's Vineyard arrived on the scene in his little fishing sloop, the thirty-two-foot *Priscilla*, which was powered by motor and sail. Sometime after daylight, a short lull in the great storm allowed the *Priscilla* to penetrate the freezing fog using only steam power. As the *Priscilla* had a shallow draft, it was able to reach the sinking vessel. The fishermen approached in the *Priscilla*'s dories. They

Mertie B. Crowley at sea. *Historic New England.*

got leeward of the wreck and anchored. The seamen got everyone out of the rigging as the sea pounded the ship to pieces. Everyone on board was successfully rescued. The five members of the *Priscilla*'s crew each received a bronze Carnegie medal and significant cash awards. Various relics of the *Crowley* were salvaged and are scattered about the Vineyard. They include both the ship's forty-six-star American flag and the owner's flag—MBC in white letters against a blue and red background—which is in the Martha's Vineyard Museum.

The explanation for the *Mertie B. Crowley*'s demise speaks to the problem of such a huge sailing ship, as apparently the planks buckled in heavy seas so that sea water had to be pumped to keep the hold free of water.

The first and only seven-masted schooner, the *Thomas W. Lawson*, was launched from Quincy, Massachusetts, in 1902. The initial plans by designer Bowdoin B. Crowninshield were for eight masts. The ship, which had a steel hull, was built as a coal carrier and later became a transatlantic oil carrier.

Chapter 6

Red Jacket

The era of the majestic clipper ships coincided with a booming U.S. economy. From the 1840s until the mid-1850s, many could pay top dollar for China tea, and then, during the gold rush, carrying provisions, the clippers made their way from the East Coast and through to the "Golden Gate" of San Francisco. Several hundred of their design were built; exactly how many depends on the definition.

They were the racehorses of the sea—long and lean with exceptionally tall masts and acres (sometimes as many as twenty) of sails, concave forward hulls with knife-edged bows and the widest beam over halfway back the ship. Clippers can be seen only in photographs and paintings, and none were among the tall ships that dazzled New Yorkers when they sailed into New York Harbor and up the Hudson for the 1976 bicentennial celebration. Ten of these racehorses of the sea were built in Rockland, and one of them, the *Red Jacket*, set the speed record crossing the Atlantic Ocean, going from New York to Liverpool in a record thirteen days, one hour and twenty-five minutes in 1854 on its maiden voyage.

Samuel Hartt Pook, a Boston-based naval architect, designed the *Red Jacket*, his fifth clipper. His was a family business with his father, who designed ironclad ships for Civil War river campaigns; theirs had the improbable name of Pook & Pook. The *Red Jacket* had a crew of sixty-five and was captained by Asa Eldridge, whom Cornelius Vanderbilt had previously chosen to captain his fabled yacht *North Star*.

Red Jacket by Percy A. Sanborn. *Penobscot Marine Museum.*

Two stories of brothers are connected with the ship. First, its name came from co-owner Isaac Taylor and was a nickname that white settlers applied to Sagoyewatha ("he who keeps awake"). This famed Seneca leader and orator had aided the Crown during the French and Indian War and for his services as a messenger was given a red jacket, which he wore often—hence the nickname. He got one of Taylor's relatives released after the British captured him. The spokesman for the Iroquois Confederacy in 1792, Sagoyewatha led forty-nine other chiefs to Philadelphia, where they agreed to mediate in the frontier war. Throughout his life, Sagoyewatha promulgated a path of strength for the Six Nations by maintaining the traditional culture of their ancestors. He argued eloquently for his people to reject further depletion of their lands. For his part, Isaac Taylor vowed to memorialize his brother and the chief, a promise he kept decades later when Sagoyewatha was no longer alive.

The second story relates to George Thomas, born into a family of boat builders in 1792 in North Haven Island, then called North Island. George's brother Benjamin was lost at sea in one of their boats, the *Thomas*. The next year, George married Peggy Vinal, whose father was one of the original incorporators of the Fox Islands, as were George's forebears. The couple moved to Rockland, where Benjamin's widow joined them. George became known as Deacon because of his devotion to the Baptist Church. In silent memory of the loved ones he had lost, George called the first vessel he built, in 1827, the *Thomas*. Three years later, that ship with its crew of five sank a few miles from Phippsburg, Maine.

The *Red Jacket* was the last vessel built by Thomas in Maine, as he couldn't acquire the space he needed at the harbor and moved his operation to Quincy.

The *Rockland Gazette* informed readers that at the *Red Jacket*'s launch it had on its stern a carving with a central figure of "a bust of an Indian… very chastely executed by our townsman S.L. Treat." The fare for up to fifteen passengers was steep, and the appurtenances were gorgeous. The woodwork—rosewood, mahogany, satinwood, zebrawood and black walnut—was from many continents.

The *Red Jacket*, once it left from New York in January 1854, did not return to Rockland. It became the first of the White Star Line, flying the British flag. Most of its career was as a very fleet transport for settlers to Australia, after which it was a coastal carrier for lumber.

The ship does seem to have functioned as a racehorse. When it left arrived in Liverpool, all the tugboats tried to get lines aboard, but the clipper was moving too fast, so Eldridge shortened the sail and backed the *Red Jacket* into its berth.

According to the Penobscot Marine Museum's "Penobscot Bay History Online":

> *Currier's lithograph of 1855 shows the penguin's view of* Red Jacket *ghosting through the ice. Their artist must have used artistic license and*

possibly the line drawing later published in the US Nautical Journal *for data. One of her passengers publishing in London, gave a highly descriptive account, citing the captain and second mate aloft, conning the ship through the ice, and remarking on icebergs "most grand."*

Two years after Asa Eldridge sailed the *Red Jacket* from New York to Liverpool, he was captain of the USM *Pacific*, one of the first steam-powered ocean liners, when it disappeared in the North Atlantic in an extremely cold winter, it was assumed from colliding with an iceberg.

Chapter 7

Before *Kon-Tiki*

Captain Albert W. Keller (1832–1914) was born and raised in Rockland. He can't have had much time at home, as he was perpetually off to sea. He began as a sailor and became, successively, the captain of a schooner, several brigs and several barks, traveling on the Panama and Pacific routes until he took command of the *Elizabeth Kimball*, sailing on this clipper ship for seven years. On March 14, 1873, the *Elizabeth Kimball* left Port Gamble, Washington, bound for Chile. But six hundred miles from Easter Island, the ship sprang a leak. The deck load of lumber was jettisoned, but still the ship went down. With fifteen feet of water in the eighteen-foot hold, abandoning the ship became the only alternative, and on May 6, the captain ran it ashore on the barren edges of Easter Island. Part of the rigging and sails were saved, along with provisions.

They were met by the despot of the island, a Frenchman named Jean-Baptiste Dutrou-Bornier. This man was a usurper of power on Easter Island, a mariner who had escaped from murder charges in South America. He was getting rich by turning Easter Island into one big ranch for sheep and other livestock. Dutrou-Bornier was a contemptable person. He chased away Native people to other islands and kidnapped young girls. (He had left behind a wife and children in France and stolen a man's wife on Easter Island, whom he proclaimed his queen.) France was not embracing the tyrant and bully's concept of Easter Island as a protectorate with him as ruler, but he was, at that juncture, still trying.

The cargo of the *Elizabeth Kimball* was a total loss, so the shipwrecked captain; his wife, Laura; and the crew members must have taken handouts from Dutrou-Bornier, but mostly they had enough provisions. Dutrou-Bornier himself had meat to spare, as he owned four thousand sheep, seventy cattle, twenty horses, three hundred pigs and many chickens.

Meanwhile, another ship, named the *William and Thomas*, had a similar mishap on its journey from the state of Washington to Chile. It likewise sprang a leak, and pumping was to no avail. On March 5, 1873, the *William and Thomas* became so waterlogged five hundred miles from Easter Island that its captain changed course for Easter Island, beaching there on March 18. From this ship, the crew saved rigging, sails and apparently a large quantity of water-damaged lumber.

Over the next several months, the seamen built a ten-ton schooner from the wrecks. At the end of the least stormy and coolest month, on July 29, Albert and Laura Keller and seven crew members of the two wrecked ships left for Tahiti. They sailed 2,550 miles, a passage of twenty-four days. Those who knew Captain Keller were amazed to see him living.

The first mate, Patrick Calligan, was an independent-minded fellow who chose to go his own way. He constructed a smaller boat and arrived a few weeks after the first boat. The remainder of the ships' crews were eventually taken off the island by a steamer sent to their aid. Calligan, however, decided to live in Tahiti. He took charge of a schooner that made rounds between Tahiti and other nearby islands, but he was killed by a cook aboard a schooner he was captain of in 1875. It is unknown whether the Kellers intended to get home to the east. Laura died in the aftermath of delivering stillborn twins and is buried with them in a Port Gamble, Washington cemetery. Due to all the lumber that had floated up on their shore, the Easter Islanders changed from huts to houses.

The despot's wife, the mother of his two "princesses," who was a seamstress, decided a few years after that it was not worth putting up with him. Legend has it that the issue that erupted was his unwillingness to buy her promised dress fabrics. Encouraged by the wife, adversaries killed him.

That the schooner was built on Easter Island remains an astonishment; it was accomplished by fitting a surviving lifeboat with masts and riggings.

Chapter 8
Hiram G. Berry

Hiram Gregory Berry, born in 1824, was the fourth of five children of Jeremiah and Frances Gregory of Rockland. Their farm was on West Meadow Road, and a life of working the farm was cut out for Hiram. He voiced a desire to attend West Point; however, his mother did not want a son in the military and thwarted him. His parents insisted he learn carpentry, and Hiram turned into a master of the trade. He built a number of residences while a young man, including his house at the corner of Beech and White Streets, and the Second Baptist Church. In 1848, he established a lumberyard. He was elected to the state legislature in 1852 and served as Rockland's second mayor (Rockland having separated from Thomaston). He married Almira Brown, and they had a child, Lucy.

According to *The Shore Village Story*, he was defeated at the next election by Charles Crockett and returned to business, founding a steam manufacturing company that made doors, sashes and blinds. He also became a director and then president of the Lime Rock Bank.

When the Civil War began, Hiram Berry went to Augusta and offered his services to Governor Washburn. He was given orders to recruit a regiment and came home. He entrusted his lumberyard to William H. Glover and raised the Fourth Maine Regiment from Rockland, Belfast, Damariscotta, Winterport and Wiscasset. Colonel Berry drilled the men in May and June 1861; their encampment was at the top of Tillson's Hill between Middle and Rankin Streets. They slept in small white tents of sailcloth, with flooring several inches off the ground, and the camp utensils were made by J.C. Libby

Monument to General Hiram G. Berry in Achorn Cemetery. *Nasser K.*

& Son of Rockland. Going in, the troops did not have uniforms. They were originally enlisted for three months but were asked to reenlist for three years, although some refused. The regimental banner was inscribed "From the Home of Knox." On June 17, they left by a steamboat bound for Portland, thence by train to Washington, D.C.

Berry fought in the First Battle of Bull Run, Yorktown and Williamsburg, and for his brave service, he was promoted to brigadier general in April

1862. He was reassigned to the command of the Third Brigade of the Third Division of the Third Army Corps, which was composed of three Michigan regiments and one New York. Berry's brigade fought in the Battle of Seven Pines. He was promoted to major general on November 29, 1862, and placed in command of the Army of the Potomac, the Second Division of the Third Army Corps.

In the wake of the Seven Days Battles in June 1862, exhausted and indomitable, Berry wrote home that he had been bruised when his horse was shot and fell on him,

> *but am not injured so badly but that I can do my daily duty. Out of some 4,400 men that I have had in my command since I joined the brigade, I now have less than 1,500. The dead lie on six different battle fields and some half-dozen places where we have had skirmishes. This army is now much reduced. We are getting reinforcements daily, and will soon be right again. I am not well tonight I shall try to recruit my health if possible.*

There were many accounts of Berry's valor, tirelessness and modesty. He did not sleep in a tent all month but instead with his horse's reins in his hands. Régis de Trobriand was a Frenchman from Tours who became a naturalized American citizen and rose to general during the Civil War. He was a colonel when he met Berry, and he wrote in *Four Years with the Army of the Potomac* (1867) this impression of him:

> *I called on General Berry with the order assigning the fifty-fifth to his command. He was a plain, straight-forward man, tall and broad-shouldered. His blue flannel blouse and his whole dress gave him very little of a military air. But whoever judged him from his appearance would have judged badly, for, although he had rather the appearance of an honest farmer than that of a brigadier-general, he was not the less a good officer, as faithful to his duty as he was devoted to his soldiers.*

At the Battle of Chancellorsville, Berry died by a sharpshooter's shot from a long distance on the morning of May 3, 1863, halfway through the war. Berry was remembered for good judgment, unflagging energy and manifesting great coolness in battle. His funeral was held in a field opposite his house, where five to six thousand people gathered, including the fifteenth vice president of the United States, Hannibal Hamlin of Bangor, Maine. Some criticized the vice president for not speaking in his official capacity.

Berry Manor Inn. *Nasser K.*

Hamlin explained that his sadness was too profound to express in formal consolation. The procession went down Limerock Street and up Main and North Main Streets to the Achorn Cemetery at Blackington's Corner. Four white horses led the funeral car, and General Berry's own three horses were led behind it. The horse he had ridden in battle, equipped as when the general dismounted from him a few minutes before his death, was led by a young man who had been in the general's service.

Franklin Simmons of Webster, Maine, was commissioned as early as that year to create a life-size memorial to General Berry. The cemetery site was semiprivate, and the memorial was to console his family and honor his state and country. Before this, Simmons, age twenty-four, had been doing portraits. His beautiful statue, which honored a local victim of the war, became a forerunner for sculptures in public places in Maine and elsewhere in the country. The statue presents Berry gazing into the distance in a martial attitude and is modeled to look like the real person while having a neo-Classical idealism. Next, Simmons did commemorative statues in public places for Lewiston, Maine, and Chelsea, Massachusetts. In late 1864, he began a series of twenty-four medallions that included portraits of Ulysses S. Grant, Admiral David Farragut and Secretary of State William Seward. They were in profile like Roman cameos and were exhibited in Washington, New York, Chicago and Philadelphia. President Lincoln promised Simmons to sit for his bust two days before he was killed. In 1908, the sculptor described himself as most likely the only American sculptor who remembered the president. Simmons did two important commissions in Washington, D.C.: the forty-five-foot-tall Navy Monument honoring the role of the navy in the Civil War, which is at the foot of the Capitol, and the marble monument of Grant for the rotunda of the Capitol, placed opposite the statue of George Washington.

During his lifetime, Simmons made over one hundred busts of notable people. One of Lincoln's vice president Hannibal Hamlin is in the Capitol. Before he began it, Simmons asked Edward Clark, the architect of the Capitol, if he preferred the classical style with bare neck and draping or the naturalistic style with frock coat, collar and necktie, to which Clark replied, "I have not much sympathy for the frock coat." Simmons made the statue in his studio in Rome, but before he sailed to Europe, he went to visit Hannibal Hamlin in Maine. Hamlin preferred the frock coat to classical garb, and this is how the sculptor portrayed him.

Chapter 9
Davis Tillson

The Tillson House, 157 Talbot Avenue, was constructed in 1853 in the Carpenter Gothic style. The National Register of Historic Places describes the Tillson House as a villa reduced to cottage scale. Two and a half stories, with a cross-gabled roof and wooden trim, it is unusual in Maine for being built of brick. When the house was built in 1853, brick making was a relatively new industry locally, and houses were built of wood. Today, this private house has grounds beautifully kept up, and the exterior has several points of architectural interest. Jigsaw ornamentations, called vergeboards, are attached to the gables. A porch supported by columns projects in front of the large eastern gable. The windows of the house have granite sills and lintels, and the windows nearest the gable peaks are in the form of Gothic arches and also have granite sills.

The house was built for Rockland's notable serial entrepreneur Davis Tillson (1830–1895), the grandson of an innkeeper. He studied hard and was appointed to West Point in 1849, but his second year at the Academy, he suffered a serious puncture wound. The injury required amputation of his left foot, and he went home to recover. He was readmitted to West Point on crutches, but when his father died, he resigned and took over the family affairs. In 1852, Tillson married Margaret Achorn, and they had two daughters, Jennie and Monira. He was elected to the state legislature as the candidate from the new antislavery Republican Party and was named the state's adjutant general. Abraham Lincoln appointed him the collector

General Davis Tillson's house at the top of Middle Street Hill (now Talbot Avenue). *Rockland Historical Society.*

of customs in July 1961. He also helped drill Captain Hiram G. Berry's local militia unit, the Rockland City Guards.

This was the same July when the South routed the North in the first big battle of the Civil War at Bull Run. Had Davis Tillson only done this one thing in his life, he would still be an amazing example of courage and fortitude due to his response to that defeat: Tillson resigned as collector of customs to join the army. Apparently, before he showed up at the mustering station, he discovered that the officer in charge had been a West Point classmate, who might reject him as unsound for service. He raised his doubts with his friend Neal Dow, the famed abolitionist, who was the colonel of the Thirteenth Maine Volunteers. Despite Dow's reassurance that Tillson, who had been fitted with a prosthetic a decade before, walked so well that nobody would suspect, Dow went with Tillson to the muster in case he needed to speak up for his friend's soundness. But it was unnecessary. The old classmate said, "I know you. I would pass you if you had lost both legs and arms." Tillson joined up as a captain of the Second Maine Artillery Battery.

He drilled his regiment in Portland that winter, and in April 1861, their first assignment was to the Department of the Rappahannock under

General McDowell. As a major, Tillson fought at Cedar Mountain and became McDowell's chief of artillery. Promoted to brigadier general in March 1863, he supervised the defense of Cincinnati and the Louisville-Nashville Railroad. In the winter of 1863, he was in command of Knoxville when General Ulysses S. Grant visited. Tillson presented him with a request to recruit soldiers in order to form a heavy artillery unit of men of color to defend Knoxville. By an order of January 6, 1864, the request was granted to recruit soldiers under Brigadier General Tillson to form an artillery regiment of "troops of African descent" (also referred to as the "Colored Infantry"). Under Tillson, this force shored up the fortifications in Tennessee and was sent to Asheville as well. Tillson wrote to the adjutant general of Maine of his great pride in "4,000 troops of all kinds," 1,000 of whom he worked with daily and who had impressed General Sherman. By the end of the war, there were 175 so-called United States Colored Troops, disbanded in peacetime.

The sack of Asheville by Union troops in April 1865 aggravated local people's anger at the occupation. They were especially enraged that Black troops were involved in governing them. When a report came of the rape of a young white woman and the assault of her old uncle and aunt at a farm ten miles north of Asheville, the blame fell on four Black soldiers in the vicinity.

Tillson's Wharf. *Penobscot Marine Museum.*

Tillson's Wharf in the snow. *Rockland Historical Society*.

As all four belonged to the First U.S. Colored Heavy Artillery, organized by Tillson, satisfaction was demanded of him.

White women of the North or South had to be safe; given the severity of the crime, Tillson ordered a firing squad to execute the four men. A Confederate brigadier general named Robert B. Vance, who later became a congressman, informed his brother Zebulon that the men were executed in his field. Zebulon Vance would serve two terms as North Carolina's governor and one in the U.S. Senate. Right after the Civil War, Tillson was briefly called back to military service to head the Freedmen's Bureaus in Tennessee and Georgia.

After the war, Tillson expanded his businesses in many directions. He was the proprietor of both granite and lime industries in the city of Rockland. He built the largest wharf in the city. He was known to be a tough manager as well as a business genius. When he and his wife began to spend winters in Florida, he bought orange groves and vegetable farms there to raise cabbages and potatoes. He was ambitious and dauntless. He was known to come to his quarries on Hurricane Island (off Vinalhaven) and make speeches. British granite workers dubbed him "Lord of the

Isles," and he was called "Bombast Furioso" by the Italians. Nevertheless, he was universally respected.

In the 1870s, the Tillsons moved to the corner of Maine and Talbot to a house that is no longer standing. It was Greek Revival and more ostentatious than their earlier house, with a handsome wrought-iron fence all round. The granite mausoleum at his grave in Achorn Cemetery is impressive too.

Chapter 10

Baker's Dozen

What is striking about the handsome houses of the residential section of Rockland is the variety within a small area of so much architectural enthusiasm and prettiness.

Even those in the same style are not lookalikes, as a result of awesome local carpenters who built wooden ships as well as residences all through the nineteenth century. "In civilizations without boats," writes the French philosopher Michel Foucault, "dreams dry up," and the stunning nineteenth-century houses of Rockland have a quality of fantasy or dreams that resulted from shipbuilders translating solutions from their highly refined craft to houses and public buildings. For example, ship's knees, used to brace a hull, were applied to the trusswork of timber beams framing a house's rafters or grand foyer or a church ceiling. A technique of overlaying wood planks (the archetype is seen on Viking ships), known as lapstrake, was sometimes used on siding. The legacy of shipbuilding also includes details on eaves and interior arches like on a boat's prow and widow's walks that evoke a quarterdeck. The Nichols-Sortwell House in Wiscasset has very elaborate rope molding and rounded arches that, stated Historic New England curator Peggy Konitzky, "clearly demonstrate that they were made and possibly designed by ship carpenters." Such a house's scale and elegance were designed to make a statement and impress all who looked on it.

My friend Canadian historian Ronald Rees summarizes the link between shipbuilding and architecture as follows:

> *The most obvious crossover is the heavy curved timbering of barns and church roofs, not unlike the heavy ribs of a ship skeleton. Shipwrights were used to build churches and barns. Other similarities seem confined to details. Carpenters work with straight lines and angles whereas the shipwright's world is one of bends and curves.*

Maine Preservation gave a pointer for old-house detectives in an article in *Down East* on January 31, 2018, that applies to Rockland—not to be thrown by different roof types and additions of various styles and heights: "Here in Maine, families often built onto their homes, adding a new, formal structure facing the street and/or an ell in back that connected the original residence to a barn."

No. 3 Elm Street is part of the Farnsworth Museum, a two-story clapboard Greek Revival (or Neo-Georgian) house with a low gabled roof and a decorative front entablature supported by flattened pilasters. Dating from 1850, this is a natural place to begin a residential tour, as it is a dwelling where many of the original furnishings remain. No. 3 Elm Street is, as Michael Komanecky, chief curator of the Farnsworth Museum, has said, a combination of an "austere exterior" and "boldly decorated mid-Victorian interior." William A. Farnsworth was an early president of the Rockland

Farnsworth Homestead. *Nasser K.*

Water Company, which explains the modern tin-lined wood refrigerator and the hot-water heater that circulated hot water to the upstairs bathroom.

The Federal houses where sea captains lived in New England were on Main Street in Thomaston or in Belfast, which was where the prosperous men of their era (1770–1830) lived. Then the prosperity switched to Rockland because of the lime industry. Most of the old houses in the center of Rockland and out on the main roads of the St. George Peninsula are Greek Revival in style. There are so many that they can be overlooked. They can be identified by the prominent feature of a pediment, which is a complete triangle at the ends of the gable roof, usually with pilasters, and often Greek ornamentation like Doric pilasters or dentils.

Queen Anne houses are scattered over the residential district. They include 16 Lincoln Street, 47 Masonic Street, 112 Beech Street and 88 Talbot Street, and the fanciful details, such as wood decoration under the eaves of the last, are a joy. The lifestyle of having many servants passed after the Gilded Age, but recent owners have preserved these grande dames of architecture. Next, in the few empty lots a more modern and informal architecture cropped up, the Bungalow style. Some examples by a local architect, Freeman Stanley, can be found, notably 107 and 120 Limerock Street.

The Victorian mansions are in a way masquerading because many were built by one construction company, part of whose genius was versatility. William Howe Glover (1834–1920) was the seventh of twelve children born to a carpenter who learned his trade in Pembroke, Massachusetts. In 1863, William and his younger brother Kent established the firm of W.H. Glover & Company. The residential section of downtown Rockland has its posh lineaments largely because of the Glovers. The firm, which figured prominently throughout the state, sold lumber, sash, doors, blinds, millwork and cast-iron elements, as well as architectural designs. One member of the family, Edward F. Glover, served as the company's principal architect. Each of the four Glover family members who lived in the residential district owned houses designed by the firm and either designed by or borrowed from prominent architects in the Queen Anne, Second Empire and Italianate styles. The Glover Company also built civic buildings, including the courthouse, and rustic houses with unpainted shingles for the elite on the Fox Islands.

The residential historic district encompasses Beech, Broad, Grove, Limerock, Lincoln, Maple, Masonic, Summer, Talbot and Union Streets and goes through the quiet, variegated Victorian architectural wonderland of Rockland. A stroll down any of these streets, turning right or left and back as desired, will dazzle.

Coming back to Main Street, the commercial buildings—Italianate, Greek Revival and Classical Revival—erected after the last fires of the 1850s are a pleasant subject to themselves. They go down to the Rankin Block at 600–10, a Greek Revival commercial building that faces the harbor and was used by maritime-related businesses such as ship's chandlery, shipping offices and a sail loft.

Chapter 11

Mary Brown Patten

Three young sea captains laid wagers—not unusual among sailors—as to who would get his cargo from the New York Harbor to San Francisco first. Speed was of the essence for this long trip around the southern tip of South America, as the captain who could complete the voyage from New York first received a big bonus. The year was 1856, and Joshua Patten took along his wife.

Joshua was twenty-four and Mary sixteen when they married in Rockland. At that time, Joshua was captain of a coastal schooner on the Boston to New York route. Mary went to sea and displayed a vibrant interest in navigation. She read Joshua's books and peppered him with questions. Soon Joshua got his big chance when the captain of *Neptune's Car*, a clipper ship, dropped out of his command and Joshua was engaged to take over. Mary was pregnant, and Joshua wouldn't go without her, so Joshua and Mary sailed together from New York for San Francisco in July 1856. That trip went smoothly, but their second voyage in *Neptune's Car* did not by a long shot.

Problems started when the first mate, named Tarker, began sleeping through his watch. The second mate could not handle navigation, so Joshua was doing around-the-clock duty as they approached Cape Horn. Then, suddenly, Joshua collapsed. He couldn't see, had a high fever and became delirious, at a juncture at sea that was clearly difficult under any circumstances.

So, Mary filled in and effectively assumed command of the clipper. From a well-to-do East Boston family, she had always loved to study. She set the

Mary Ann Brown Patten, sea captain. *National Portrait Gallery, Washington, D.C.*

course and navigated while tending to her sick husband. It was reported later that for a while, she had to tie him to his bunk while she carried out the duties of replacement captain. In addition, Tarker incited the other crew members to mutiny, and Mary had to persuade them to give her their trust. Joshua got a little better and returned the first mate to his watch until discovering that Tarker had changed the ship's course to Chile, possibly intending to sell the $300,000 worth of cargo in Valparaíso. So, the first mate was locked up and the captain relapsed into fever, but Mary's troubles did not end. Tarker got free and tried to assault Mary. She later recounted how she hit him over the head with the butt of a pistol and knocked him unconscious. He was dragged back into the cell, and she padlocked the door.

Mary completed the trip into port in San Francisco on the 135th day out of New York. She came in second, beating all but one of the vessels involved in Joshua Patten's wager.

The astonishing achievement of the plucky captain's wife was a news story that traveled the world. She didn't change her clothes for fifty days! She could not disguise her pregnancy from the unruly crew! She was so good at navigation that she knew to drop the sails off the Horn for three days during a gale!

Joshua, who was a Mason, received help from the California Masonic Temple, which sent someone to accompany him back to Boston. Mary was awarded a bonus of $1,000 from the shipping line, and a Boston newspaper set up a fund for the Pattens to pay for Joshua's medical expenses. Mary claimed only to have done a wife's plain duty to a good husband. Mary had her baby but died shortly after her husband when she was only twenty-three. Their four-year-old son went to live with Joshua's parents in Rockland.

Chapter 12
Young Mechanic

Mechanic Street is tucked away in the South End of town. Its small antique houses are shipshape and comely. They have a view of the harbor, and at the end of the street, young people learn boating at the Sail Power and Steam Museum. While the street's name suggests a person whose occupation involved machinery, a mechanic originally meant anyone who worked with tools, and the street was named in recognition of a shipbuilding prodigy.

Most of the great ships of Maine were built in small boatyards; nevertheless, building a large vessel required a costly investment. Francis W. Rhoades had already built two clipper ships when he took the design of his third from a model whittled by his son, William. In William's honor, he called it the *Young Mechanic*. Unfortunately, when Francis had partly completed this third clipper, he was taken to the District Court of Rockland. He had missed payments on three loans adding up to $65,000 to William McLoon of Rockland for buying materials and paying wages. Francis Rhoades conveyed the vessel to McLoon on December 4, 1855, and died suddenly four days later. Rhoades's son, eighteen-year-old William, carried on and completed the construction, on which basis he fully merits being called a prodigy.

The *Young Mechanic* proved outstanding. It made a crossing from Savannah, Georgia, to Liverpool, England, in 17 days, sailing an average of 288 miles per day. On a westward voyage, in the spring of 1862, it rounded Cape Horn from New York and arrived in San Francisco in 127 days. However, the ship

Young Mechanic, painting by James G. Babbidge of Rockland. *Rockland Historical Society, photograph by Ann Morris.*

had reversals. After carrying coal to San Francisco in the fall of 1864, it was damaged by gales and had to be docked for repairs in St. Thomas. That winter, subject to storm damage again, the *Young Mechanic* aborted its course and put into Newport, Rhode Island, whence it sailed to Boston to repair the masts and hull.

In May, under charter to Tudor & Company, the *Young Mechanic* took a cargo of ice to India. Charles W. McLoon, age thirty-two, son of the ship's owner, captained the ship. Along with the second mate and three crewmen, Charles contracted cholera in Madras and died. The first mate, G.T. Richardson, took charge of the ship sailing back to Boston. It arrived on January 28, 1866, carrying the embalmed body of Charles McLoon.

Tudor & Company chartered the ship again. On March 5, 1866, it sailed from Boston for Hong Kong with a cargo of ice, pitch and kerosene under the command of Captain William Grant. But the ship was set on fire a month later in the South Atlantic and sank in a few hours. The eighteen crew members and twenty-six passengers were rescued by the French vessel *Eugenie* and dropped off at Pernambuco, Brazil. There the case went before the American Council. First Mate Edward Perkins testified that he knew the plot two weeks before the arson occurred.

In *The Clipper Ships of Rockland, Maine*, Gene Barron and Andrew Carpenter summarize the course of what devolved:

> *Perkins stated that he spoke to Captain Grant about his intention to burn the ship and that William Grant told him the ship was "always unfortunate that she was insured, was deficient in matters of outfit and that there was an understanding with the owner that she should not go to Hong Kong." Initially Perkins said that he objected to the plan but later consented to join in because he was fearful of retaliation should he refuse to cooperate. Accordingly the boats were outfitted with stores and the vessel was set alight on April 6 or 7.*

The council made a judgment that the *Young Mechanic* had indeed been destroyed on purpose.

When First Mate Edward Perkins returned to Rockland, he informed William McLoon of the miscreance for which Captain Grant had been responsible. Captain Grant, charged with burning his ship, was released on $30,000 bail, which was "furnished." The conclusion of the September trial was that the jury found Captain Grant not guilty.

The Rockland Historical Society displays marine artist James G. Babbidge's portrait of the *Young Mechanic*, given to the society by Barbara Hagen, the great-granddaughter of McLoon. In retrospect, the owner of the ship, William McLoon, more than the ship, seems to have been unlucky. William's son Charles W. McLoon, who was the ship captain who died in India, lies in Rockland's Achorn Cemetery.

Chapter 13
Rescue at Owls Head

Owls Head Lighthouse, dramatically perched on a cliff one hundred feet over the water, is a formidable sight. However, children can relate to the story of "Spot the Dog," the springer spaniel that lived there in the 1930s, whose monument is at the base of the tower. Spot performed vital acts of devotion. The keeper's children taught him to ring the fog bell by tugging on its rope with his teeth each time he heard a ship's whistle. The skipper of the mailboat was Spot's friend; one terrible night when the mailboat was lost in a blizzard, Spot guided the skipper home.

Lighthouse stories are fascinating because they recount how people have mastered dire situations, including loneliness and death-defying storms. Various sources, including Bill Caldwell's *Islands of Maine*, tell the following story of an insane shipwreck involving the Owls Head keeper from long ago.

It begins with a monstrous gale of December 22, 1850—"one of the most terrible storms we have ever witnessed," wrote the *Lime Rock Gazette*. Five ships were lost along the eight-mile stretch between Owls Head and Spruce Head. One was a small coasting schooner from Massachusetts at anchor at Jameson's Point north of Rockland Harbor. The captain had gone ashore while the mate, Richard B. Ingraham; his fiancée, Lydia Dyer; and one deckhand named Roger Elliot were aboard, all asleep. The plan was for the schooner to return to Boston the following day.

At midnight, the anchor lines snapped, and the schooner blew across Penobscot Bay toward Owls Head, where it smashed on the ledges south of the lighthouse. Water poured into the hold, but the vessel held fast to the

Cove at Owls Head. *Nasser K.*

ledges and did not sink. The mate, his bride-to-be and the deckhand crept under blankets they brought up onto the deck.

As surf and waves sloshed over the three people, coats of ice built up on them all night. It is noted that the deckhand used a knife and his fists to keep a breathing hole open. By 6:00 a.m., he decided their best chance was if he made for the keeper's house on shore. He struggled upward over the ledges to the dirt road, where he was spied either from the kitchen or, according to another account, by the keeper who happened to be going by on his sleigh. The seaman, Roger Elliot, was rushed into the warm house. Before collapsing, as soon as the seaman could speak, he explained there were two more people still on the boat. Then the keeper, William Masters, formed a rescue party of ten men (how he notified them in the not very populated

Owls Head Lighthouse. *Nasser K.*

Baptist churchwomen playing in the surf at Crescent Beach, 1890s. *Rockland Historical Society.*

Owls Head is not clear). The frozen block of the bodies of bridegroom and bride was brought from the deck of the schooner to the house. The pair was, to all appearances, dead. The keeper poured water over the ice that encased them, slowly increasing the water temperature while the rescue party massaged and exercised the bodies' frozen limbs. Three hours later, the couple revived to consciousness. Ingraham opened his eyes and asked, "What is all this? Where are we?"

To those on hand, it must have been as though the three people came back from the dead. Weeks later, they could walk. The brave deckhand only partially recovered, but miraculously, Richard Ingraham and Lydia Dyer regained their health. They married six months later, in June, and had four children.

Chapter 14

Charivaris

In eighteenth-century England, the opposing sides in parliamentary elections were even more partisan, and more given to brawling, than football (soccer) supporters today. In one of William Hogarth's *Election Series* paintings (1755), a Tory candidate has won and is being carried aloft on a chair in a mêlée of celebrants. But one of his supporters has accidentally hit another one, bearing the chair, on the head with a stick, and the victor is about to be flung to the ground. Hogarth's Whig assailant is a sailor, and a Tory victor has lost his hand and fights with a hook. Class divisions were behind brawls in North America, too, often as not.

Men often joined in the ruckus not from being staunch followers of a candidate or policy but more on the spur of the moment from solidarity with their peers. A burgess in Shrewsbury in the 1770s lost his eye jumping into such a fight. The newspaper made very little of the injury, and he was admired for his spontaneity, energy and valor. Charivaris are especially associated with the French and were ubiquitous at country weddings among the Acadians. But in St. John, New Brunswick, the upper-class Loyalists, many of them Harvard graduates and lawyers, were so disturbed by a plebian mob that they managed to push most of them out of the city, making it years before the democratically persuaded had a voice in Canada.

From the late eighteenth through mid-nineteenth centuries, these political expressions were in the tradition of a lighter local amusement, the shivaree, or charivari, staged at weddings or festivals. A charivari involved costumes and props, noise and raucous singing.

"Horribles" at a Fourth of July parade. The goat is in the coach. *Marshall Point Lighthouse/ Aidan Kaczynski.*

Camden had a charivari called the Antiquities and Horribles in 1833 when a band of citizens judged that the U.S. government should do more to protect the coast without drafting their sons. In 1848, Rockland had a major scuffle that also took the form of a charivari, with residents showing their displeasure by demonstrating dressed up and armed with outrageous farm implements.

On the other hand, there is a photograph of a long-ago July 4 charivari in Port Clyde that suggests the celebrants were having pure fun: a goat peeks out from the stagecoach that used to carry mail from Port Clyde to Thomaston.

In 1854, Rockland was applying to the state to be a city. As a town, it had made laws at an annual meeting at which townspeople voted. It had already split off from Thomaston and been named East Thomaston, switching to Rockland. But lime business and associated shipbuilding were big businesses, and now Rockland requested incorporation as a city—that would have elected council members make the laws. But the people of the quiet Blackington's Corner wanted to govern their own community. Old County Road developed before the Shore Village and Main Street, and Blackington's Corner was on the stage route from Thomaston to Camden. Besides farms, Blackington's Corner had a small mercantile center for groceries and provisions and many blacksmith shops and a carriage shop, starting where Old County Road now crosses Route 17 to where the hill rises to Dodge Mountain. John Bird petitioned to divide the locality into two: the city (Shore Village and Main Street) and the more rural town, to be called Blackington's Corner.

The population was limited in the harbor area by the fact that everyone needed their own access to the water, and properties were narrow but very long. John Bird and others argued that those who lived along the harbor would derive greater benefit from taxes imposed on the farms for new streets, city water and fire protection than he and others who lived at Blackington's Corner. The rural area, about two-thirds of the city, petitioned the state for permission to cede from Rockland and form a new town. Timothy Williams, the owner of a large lime quarry in the meadows that he wished to stay part of the new city, pushed for the unified Rockland, and arguments against Bird's petition carried. At the town meeting on June 3, 1854, the city was incorporated by a two-to-one margin. Celebrations ensued, and Knott Crockett was elected the first city mayor. However, during the Fourth of July parades, the residents of Ward 7 continued to display their displeasure for several years.

Ann Morris writes in *A History of Blackington's Corner and the Highlands* (2015):

> *Dressed in outrageous costumes and brandishing antique and horrible farm instruments, weapons, and fire-equipment, the ludicrous procession marched into the city between nine and ten o'clock and joined the parade at Limerock Street and Union. The parade, including the Rockland City Band, the City Guards, the Mechanics' Rifles, the fire engines, and various dignitaries, proceeded to Lindsey Grove where there was a reading of the Declaration of Independence and a picnic. The "Fantasticks" returned to Blackington's Corner where they dined at the house of John Bird.*

Chapter 15

Breakwater

The closest thing to walking on water for anyone reasonably surefooted is the Rockland Breakwater. For 4,346 feet, the great granite blocks, as though laid by giants, create a path across the harbor's broad mouth. The Breakwater Lighthouse lies at the southern end of this seawall, dramatically located in the middle of the harbor. Singer-songwriter Lenny Arey in his 2019 album *White Sails–Blue Water–Grey Granite–Blue Grass* captures the delight of walking on the Breakwater:

> *If you're bored go for a walk*
> *Rockland has its own boardwalk*
> *Seven-eighths of a mile and made of stone*
> *Great with company or go it alone.*

The plan was approved in 1890, and the U.S. Army Corps of Engineers in conjunction with Rockland's W.H. Glover Company built the breakwater between 1881 and 1900. Two years later, the lighthouse was lit for the first time. It had two keepers from the U.S. Coast Guard; in 1964, it was automated.

In the 1850s, the shore of Rockland received devastating damage repeatedly. The breakwater succeeded in keeping the harbor safe and navigable for traveling vessels and protected the city's maritime industries. Before it was built, severe storms not only were damaging the limekiln sheds where limestone was converted to building materials but were also

Rockland Breakwater. *Nasser K.*

causing fires along the shore (the limekiln fires were never allowed to go out). Whether transporting lime, granite or fish, Rockland has always been one of the busiest harbors in Maine.

Walking from land across the harbor on the breakwater is a unique and hypnotic experience. The Bodwell Granite Company used 700,000 tons of granite in the breakwater. The blocks were set in end to end in water up to seventy feet deep. The locally quarried granite blocks are so huge they look like a giant's neatly stacked toys. The views are panoramic—of ships, ferries and marine life. Walking the breakwater feels like being a boat sailing the distance. In season, a reward awaits those who complete the mile: a museum and the chance to gain entrance to the little gambrel-roofed frame keeper's house and square brick lighthouse tower. This was what was called a "stag" station, meaning that the keeper lived with his family on land and arrived by boat two miles across the Rockland Harbor.

At the site of the lighthouse, the breakwater is 65 feet deep, 42 feet wide on top and 175 feet wide at the bottom. According to New England Lighthouses website, "In the early years the fog signal was sounded as many as 900 hours during the year, or more than ten percent of the time."

After the lighthouse was automated, it became run-down until a chapter of the American Lighthouse Foundation was organized as the Friends of the Rockland Breakwater Lighthouse, which has restored the building. The volunteers also care for the Owls Head Lighthouse. When the exterior of

View of Rockland Breakwater. *Nasser K.*

the Breakwater Lighthouse was scraped and painted in 1999, the team of volunteers included sailors from a visiting U.S. Navy destroyer, the USS *Stump*. The paint was donated by the local Sherwin-Williams paint store, and restaurants provided meals to the volunteers.

To get to the breakwater, you take a right on Waldo and a quick right on Samoset. Walking it is exhilarating and heady, except when there is ice or big waves slosh up. Then it is not advisable.

Chapter 16

Effie's Lullaby

The melody for "Rock-a-Bye Baby" was written by Effie Carlton, an actress of the Victorian era. She recalled the words from *Mother Goose's Melody*, which had various editions, especially in New England. One summer, as a young girl of fifteen, Effie I. Crockett of Rockland (1857–1940) visited Winthrop, Massachusetts, on summer holiday with her family. She was over on the piazza of their friends' cottage and reading a book—perhaps *The Tragedy of Romeo and Juliet*—when she noticed a baby bawling in a hammock next door. She didn't know the mother's name but knew she was from Lawrence. Effie went over and, to soothe the baby, composed a melody.

When her banjo teacher back in Rockland heard her song, he encouraged her to publish it, and it became instantly popular sheet music. The lullaby is a waltz. Effie later said that she used her grandmother's surname of Canning because of concern that her parents, Edward and Jennie Crockett, might disapprove of the notoriety of her being a songwriter. She gave a different version to the *Baltimore Sun* (May 28, 1939): "I wasn't much impressed with the song, you see, and I didn't want it traced to me if it didn't fare well." Both versions, you will see, conceal the name of her first husband.

Effie's mother was fourteen and a half when she married William Edward Crockett. William was the first cousin of Charles Spofford Crockett (1830–1911), the mayor of Rockland for one year. Effie, the mayor's first cousin once removed, was probably born on the other side of the blanket.

Effie Crockett Canning. *Rockland Historical Society.*

At the age of seventy-five, William Crockett was well known as a marathoner and the writer of many newspaper and magazine articles on health. He contributed several interesting stories on the art of keeping fit to the *Globe* and always stood ready, even while approaching eighty, to defend his laurels in swimming and running against "contenders."

William Crockett gained fame. He served in the Fourth Maine Infantry all through the Civil War, rising to the rank of sergeant. At first after the move to Boston, he was in partnership dealing in liquors, but when he died, his obituary listed him as a physician.

At twenty-four, Effie married Dr. John F. Canning, a young doctor from St. John, New Brunswick, whom I suspect was an assistant of her father. Canning is the surname she used in connection with publishing the lullaby, but she was unattached seven years later. Although the marriage record (1881) of Effie and Canning states he was a physician, the death record (1888) states he was a laborer. That same year, Effie married in Boston Harry G. Carlton, an actor, and henceforth used his surname. This was a match of two performers. She toured in vaudeville shows with well-known stars. A *Boston Globe* article of January 9, 1938, states that she made her professional debut at twenty-one and played the leading part in *Shiloah* at the Old Boston Theater and in New York. Other roles of note were with William Gillette in *The Private Secretary*, with which she toured the country for forty weeks, and in *Oliver Twist*. But the plays she acted in were overshadowed by her fame as the composer of "Rock-a-Bye Baby."

Harry's obituary praised him as one of America's best-known character actors, who began his stage career at eighteen and was popular for many years, appearing in many plays with Leslie Carter and David Warfield. He was in the ensemble of a *Camille*-like play in 1911 and made a last appearance on stage with Guy Bates Post in *Omar the Tentmaker*. After retiring from the stage, he became active in motion pictures. After Harry died, Effie gave up acting. Perhaps she had a small role when he was in a movie, uncredited. She told the *Globe* reporter that her father died a few months after Harry, leaving her an only child with no immediate relatives. "I decided I had enough of the stage and retired. Now I am quite happy and never miss the stage. I have books, friends and plenty of hobbies and am able to get along quite comfortably."

Nevertheless, she was not in funds when the copyright to the song lapsed. A Massachusetts congressman, Lawrence Connery, asked Congress for a bill for renewal so that Carlton would not be deprived of royalties.

She and her second husband are buried at Mount Feake Cemetery in Waltham, Massachusetts.

Effie published other songs, including another lullaby, both words and music, advertised as a "Companion" to "Rock-a-Bye Baby" and preserved in Johns Hopkins University's Music Library:

> *"Safely Rocked in Mother's Arms"*
>
> *Gently, slowly to and fro,*
> *Sways the old arm chair*
> *Snow white brow and rosy cheeks*
> *Parted lips two teeth disclose.*
> *Tenderly the evening breeze*
> *Stirs the curls of golden hair…*
> *All that mother loves on earth*
> *Safe within her arms repose.*

A feature strikes me of the anecdote about how Effie came to compose the lullaby. Imagine her quitting the porch of her parents' friends where she is reading and going unbidden to another house to pick up the baby. Surprising, yes? This is surely old-time, except in rural parts of Maine. Once when the photographer of this book visited me, a top lobsterman, Ty Babbe, took him out on his boat. Afterward, Ty wanted to point out something of coastal geography to my friend. Having no map, Ty dashed with my friend up and down Ridge Road (Tenants Harbor), going into the houses of the fishermen he supposed would have a map—without a thought to knocking on the door. Ty explained it was the accepted custom among relatives and friends.

Chapter 17
Dermott Girls

In the Gilded Age, the same women who kept their heavy plumed hats on at a restaurant, suffered in whalebone stays and were impeccably submissive to their husbands also envied actresses who showed off their bodies, wore diamond aigrettes in their hair and had multiple affairs in which they turned the tables on lovers and left them begging for more. It came in handy that the actresses learned to exteriorize their femininity through acting in parts on stage. The stars played up the tropes of both ideal sweetheart and the femme fatale voracious for money and sex.

But whether the would-be stars acted or sang, drinking champagne at Delmonico's or Maxime's in their furs and décolletage did not suffice. There was often a gate: a serious role in Shakespeare. Two girls from Rockland—Jesse Dermott, born in 1874, and her sister Gertrude, five years younger, who also took the surname Elliott—jumped the gate. They became internationally famous on stage, given their combined acting ability, drive and business acumen.

Their father, Thomas Dermott, a Rockland sea captain, and his wife, Adelaide Hall Dermott, adopted a son, Thomas, when he was a child in Liverpool. Adelaide Hall died young, but she had been a schoolteacher and made sure her daughters had proper elocution and spoke French. (Jesse may have changed her given name in 1889 to Maxine to put an *x* through the letters that make Maine.) Her father took her on a long sea voyage after she got pregnant by a local boy at fourteen and lost the baby. Thereafter, she was sent to a convent in Boston. By age sixteen, Maxine was acting in a traveling

Maxine Elliott. *Rockland Historical Society.*

company. She and Gertrude were touring Australia in 1896, and Maxine married the actor who ran it.

Maxine triumphed in a thirty-year career on stage and in silent films. She became the first woman to own and operate a theater, named Maxine Elliott's Theater, at 39th and Broadway in New York. While it was rumored that her friend Pierpont Morgan paid for the theater, in fact she bought it with her careful investments.

Her friends were aristocrats and the princes of Europe. *New Yorker* writer and member of the Algonquin Round Table Alexander Woollcott reported in an article ("The Truth about Jesse Dermott") on how Maxine J. made one of her conquests. In a scene worthy of Henry James, one afternoon in the park at Marienbad (now the Czech Republic), King Edward VII of England passed in his carriage.

> *This young American woman in a dove-colored gown with puffed sleeves who, not without design, sat seemingly engrossed in a becoming book of poetry, her ruffled parasol tilted to shade the page.*
>
> *As Royalty went by, she chanced to look up from beneath the wide brim of her hat, and, for the space that a breath is held, their eyes met. Then she looked down at her book again and went on reading until, in ten minutes or so, an equerry came bowing and scraping with an invitation to dine that evening.*

While Maxine's marriages were casual affairs that did not endure, she fell madly in love with a much younger man, a Belgian tennis star, Anthony Wilding, fifteen years her junior. Wilding was killed in the First World War, and she continued to devote herself to Belgian relief.

Meanwhile, her sister Gertrude at twenty-six married one of England's foremost actors, Johnston Forbes-Robertson. George Bernard Shaw wrote the role of Caesar in his *Caesar and Cleopatra* for Sir Johnston and praised the actor as the best Hamlet of his age (he was forty-four before he played Hamlet and continued to play the role for seventeen years). Maxine's sister became Lady Forbes-Robertson and managed motherhood, having four children, including one who designed planes and one who continued in the acting profession. Gertrude was Desdemona to her husband's Othello and Ophelia to his Hamlet. She was a suffragist, and Lord Forbes-Robertson made speeches in support of the suffrage movement.

As lavish as Maxine's parties were, she did not lose her fortune and did not go insane to accumulate precious jewels or to gamble at the casino (she preferred bridge at home). Her passionate enterprise was social climbing, which she did on a grand scale, pursuing the titled and leaders of English society and the libertines of her age. She preferred the stage but was in several films, including one by the studio of her friend Charlie Chaplin. Her name was linked with countless men admired for their power and wealth.

Being a demimondaine as a career alternative ended with the First World War, when big spenders lost their fortunes and aristocrats their levity and largesse. Most of the *grandes horizontales*, as the French called them, went from lives of excess to morality tales.

After two marriages, Maxine remained single. When Lord Curzon proposed, she said, "I wouldn't marry God." In a career of thirty years, Maxine performed in fifty plays, mostly comedies (five by Shakespeare), and made two movies. Then, happily, at the height of her success, she retired to the south of France and built a home near Juan-les-Pins that she called the Chateau de l'Horizon. This white Art Deco chateau was not the fanciest property in the area because it had a railroad right behind it, but it had a superb view from its large terrace. A slide dropped her and her guests from the swimming pool to the sea. In the course of visits to her, Winston Churchill met Doris Castlerosse, who became his mistress during a slack period in his political life when he frequented the chateau from 1933 to 1936.

A biography of Maxine Elliott was written by her niece, Gertrude's daughter Diana Forbes-Robertson, and published by Viking Press. By this time, almost a quarter century had passed since her "Aunt Dettie" died suddenly in her sumptuous home, leaving instructions that her letters from admirers such as King Edward VII and J. Pierpont Morgan be burned. According to the biography, the beautiful actress was an outstanding businesswoman. Said her legal counsel, "If Maxine had been a man, Schiff would have been her secretary and Carnegie her office boy."

The sisters returned to Maine only once, during the summer years later, when Maxine, Gertrude and a cousin rented a cottage at the south end of Rockland.

Chapter 18

Edna St. Vincent Millay

The first woman to win the Pulitzer Prize for poetry was Edna St. Vincent Millay, raised in Camden but born in Rockland. An association of poetry lovers is preserving her birthplace (a double house) at 198/200 Broadway on the west side of the street coming into town.

In 1889, her parents, Cora and Henry, moved into an apartment in Rockland. Henry was descended from Isaiah Tolman, Rockland's first settler. He was from the little village of Union, where two of Edna St. Vincent's sisters were born. To make the move to Rockland, Henry took a job as a traveling salesman of men's clothing and worsted. It was said he had charm. They were soon able to move up and afford a nice two-family cottage with mahogany sliding doors between the parlor and dining room. Describing the home, Nancy Milford, a biographer of the poet, mentions Cora's piano, a smoking set for Henry's cigars, an oversized chair and also that "Cora had hemstitched and cross-stitched linen pillow shams and antimacassars in bright red to adorn every available surface. Henry's contribution was a set of deer antlers. They both agreed their new place was entirely 'D.E.'—damned elegant!"

Cora published one of her poems in *The Maine Farmer* and worked as a hairdresser. Three girls were born to Cora and Henry, and the eldest, Edna, was called Vincent. They hadn't lived in Rockland long when Cora became pregnant. She went into labor, and Henry raced off to the fetch the doctor. When he returned, the doctor, seeing the young husband's agitation,

Edna St. Vincent Millay, 1920s. *Van Vechten Trust/Art Resource.*

convinced him to go out for a cup of coffee. After ten hours of labor, the baby was born, and everyone was startled when the bells of Rockland began to peal, until they realized it was George Washington's birthday.

Cora's brother Charles Buzzell made national news when he was found having been trapped for weeks under a cotton bale in the hold of a ship. He appeared for a while at a museum in the Bowery of New York City under the rubric "The Adventurer and Evangelist."

After high school, Vincent performed her poem "Renascence" at a hotel in Camden called the Whitehall Inn. Her sister Norma was working there, and Vincent performed it at a party of the guests when she was twenty. It was so admired that it got her a scholarship to Vassar and publication, and she became famous even before she began college. The publisher who awarded her a prize for "Renascence" for some time believed she was a boy and addressed her as "Dear Sir." Eventually, Vincent replied, "It may astonish you to learn that I am no 'Esquire' at all, nor even a plan 'Mister'—in fact, that I am just an aspiring 'Miss' of twenty."

"Renascence"

All I could see from where I stood
Was three long mountains and a wood;
I turned and looked another way,
And saw three islands in a bay.
So with my eyes I traced the line
Of the horizon, thin and fine,
Straight around till I was come
Back to where I'd started from;
And all I saw from where I stood
Was three long mountains and a wood.

Millay House Rockland, 198–200 Broadway, Millay's birthplace. *Ann Morris.*

All her life, the poet exhibited an attitude of sensuality and candor and a very literary style. One of her most famous short poems is imbued with her spirit of rebellion that appealed to the flapper era:

> *"First Fig"*
>
> *My candle burns at both ends;*
> *It will not last the night;*
> *But ah, my foes, and oh, my friends—*
> *It gives a lovely light!*

Since 2016, a nonprofit organization, the Millay House Rockland, launched by the Rockland Historical Society, has cared for her birthplace.

Chapter 19

Edward Hopper

Edward Hopper is admired for his indelible and striking compositions. Frozen in a moment of time, his scenes suggest a mystery to unravel, yet they are the epitome of historic record.

In the summer of 1926, Edward and Jo, married two years, went to Maine. They started in Eastport, but Edward wanted a certain ethos, so they quickly picked up sticks for Rockland. On July 6, he wrote to his dealer, Frank Rehn, "We left [Eastport] after three days and went to Bangor by rail and then by boat to this town, a very fine old place with lots of good-looking houses but not much shipping."

Here, Hopper had one of the most productive seasons in his career. He painted schooners and trawlers and scenes of the waterfront, limestone quarries outside town, railroad crossings and the site of the Civil War encampment for the Fourth Maine Regiment (between Talbot and Rankin Streets). He even did a painting of the living room of the owner of the lodging house near the shipyard where they stayed. Mrs. Achorn was affable and well liked; Hopper had likely heard of her establishment before, when he was on Monhegan painting seascapes and lighthouses in the summers from 1916 to 1919. *Mrs. Achorn's Parlor* was the name he gave his painting of her front room, detailing its organ, chair, lamp, patterned rug and old-fashioned furnishings, subjecting them to his almost ruthlessly cool yet nostalgic style.

Hopper, age forty-four, completed twenty works that summer, of which the Farnsworth Museum possesses five. All watercolors, they are some of his most important works (mostly fourteen by twenty inches). The evocative *Haunted*

Rockland Talbot House, 73 Talbot Avenue. *Nasser K.*

House, once overlooking the water at 5 South Street, is one, exemplifying the fine old house style built back seemingly haphazardly from a Colonial main dwelling. The most famous is *Talbot House*, of a commodious Victorian house at 73 Talbot Street (now part of the Berry Manor Inn). The artist identified the house in his records as a "fine white mansard." Art historian and photographer Gail Levin writes in *Hopper's Places*:

> *Hopper's vantage point for this watercolor was the front step of a house located just across this quiet street, where he probably sat with his paper and paints. In his composition, he intentionally cropped the central tower, the top of the chimney, and the base of the house, creating the sense of an imposing image continuing beyond the boundary of the paper. The style*

of this house was one that had particularly appealed to Hopper over the previous three years, beginning with his watercolor The Mansard Roof, *painted in Gloucester in 1923.*

This house with the mansard roof was built for A.F. Ames by William H. Glover in 1874. In 1905, it was sold to David Talbot, the "Omaha Ice King." Born in Rockport, Talbot returned at age forty-six with his wife and three children. An examination for a life insurance policy had convinced him he should retire, and he chose to move to Maine. That he lived a healthy life for fifteen more years was attributed to a change in climate, his rugged physique and his cutting down on business. Talbot died in his car while driving to a fishing trip in Camden. Among his activities for bettering the city of Rockland was championing the highway system. Always shrewd in business, he took the advice of a nephew who was an engineer at Eastman Kodak and invested heavily and profitably in its stock.

Talbot Street, originally Middle Street, had a name change in his honor. The house continued to belong to Talbots for many years. One of the family opened the house to many parties of the community, and the Talbots' elevator was an object of curiosity to the young people who came there as late as the 1950s, many of whom had not gone up and down in an elevator before.

The artist took a perspective that emphasizes the roofline. No. 73 Talbot Street is still standing and belongs to the inn next door, 67 Talbot, which William Glover had built for himself at the same time. Glover added a tower to his house, however, to make it grander.

A much more modest white house is the center of interest in *Railway Crossing, Rockland, Maine*, in the middle of a block of Broad Street heading around between Park and Pleasant Streets.

Chapter 20

The Colorful, Seamy Side

Until 1975, those sailing out in the Penobscot Bay to Monhegan Island on a mailboat might catch sight of a bald eagle, harbor seals or the legendary hermit Ray Phillips, who passed away in that year. A naturalist and fisherman who took his back-to-nature lifestyle a step further, Phillips dwelt in a driftwood shack on the cliff of tiny Manana Island a stone's throw from Monhegan. If some thought him a do-nothing, visitors were apt to discuss his viewpoint and seek his wisdom. According to his *New York Times* obituary, "Occasionally he went to Rockland, 11 miles away, for a haircut and shave, a hotel bedroom and what he called 'A night on the town.'"

After sprucing up, where did the hermit head? Up the streets of Rockland to Broadway. "Four-Way Lil" operated the laundry on Main Street and solicited when it closed for the day. The popular "Passion Pit" with its Rainbow Room was in the basement of the Thorndike Hotel. Myrtle Street had the Windsor House for bootleg liquor and the attentions of ladies of the night. On Mechanic Street near the shipyard was a brothel called the Last Chance. "The other side of the tracks" held true, as near Crescent and the railroad tracks on South Main was a brothel near the water. Ann Morris's *A History of the Point* tells that several women who lived on the Point turned to prostitution during the Great Depression: "Because of their reputations, families on the Point had to remember to turn off their front lights or they might have a lonesome sailor knocking at the door." Of course, not all these

Thorndike Hotel, corner of Main Street and Tillson Avenue, 1920s. *Rockland Historical Society.*

red-light localities functioned at once, and the exact dates of their existence would be hard to recover.

Prostitutes also hung out at the Rockland Train Station. Of course, some men were content with paying for a dance partner, and sometimes one of the fifty to one hundred sailors who came in on a ship met someone special and got married.

During Prohibition, a speakeasy in the Kimball Block on Main Street had a piano player who was the secretary at the Birds' canning factory. But that was before Phillips's time.

The area along the shore gained a typical waterfront reputation for rowdiness and prostitution. This was also where privateers got rich from being given letters of marque by the government to attack enemies and purloin their cargo through the Revolutionary period and the War of 1812.

According to Gil Merriam, during World War II, when Rockland was a navy base, the sailors said if you put a roof over Rockland, you would have one big whorehouse. Ann Morris adds, "The Point, a bustling area along Tillson Avenue and Winter Street, was home to immigrant families. It was colorful and cosmopolitan. Everyone knew each other, and they all spoke different languages. But discrimination gave the Point a reputation for the wild things going on all over Rockland."

In 1890, Lime City, as Rockland was called, had sixteen boardinghouses, ten dining rooms, six hotels and nineteen hairdressers. In his doctoral dissertation for Louisiana State University, William Fagan writes:

> *The city was, again until only recently, known for its other services; saloons and houses of ill fame flourished, especially on Sea Street (now Tillson Avenue) where workers, fishermen, sailors, and granite cutters and quarrymen from the quarry islands spent their hard-earned wages. A 1977 business guide touted the city as "muscle town filled with beauty."*

Writer Bill Caldwell in a 1988 book declared:

> *Rockland was a boom town, Barbary Coast style....On Saturday night, several hundreds of lonely men with lots of money for a fling, descended on Rockland's waterfront....It was a blazing place. More than 30 steamships and hundreds of coasting vessels plus the ships of Rockland's huge lime trade, crowded the harbor. Bars, whorehouses, gambling joints, and dance halls catered to sailors and quarrymen. Fights blazed, and jails filled. And the money poured in.*

Chapter 21

Invasion of the Klan

After the release of D.W. Griffith's nasty if cinematically powerful epic movie *The Birth of a Nation* in 1915, racists saw an opportunity to spread hate. The Ku Klux Klan reorganized in Georgia along the lines of a nativist ideology, featuring the costumes and flaming crosses that originated in that movie.

In the nineteenth century, Irish, Italians, eastern Europeans and Scandinavians immigrated to the coast of Maine in conjunction with the lime and granite industries. To this cosmopolitan character were added French Canadians and a mix of seamen who liked the area and remained. But resentment among some Protestant Yankees was capitalized on during the early 1920s, when the Ku Klux Klan had a brief burst of power and influence in the state. Anti-foreign hostilities had a history. In the 1850s, a Catholic church was burned in Bath and a Jesuit pastor, John Bapst, was tarred and feathered in Ellsworth before fleeing to Boston, where he became the first president of Boston College. Their logic was "America for Americans," and their target was immigrant workers of all kinds in the textile and paper mills, especially French Canadians.

That movie came out in 1915, and the frightening imagery of the burning crosses and the false notion that the era of Reconstruction after the Civil War was fraught with violence perpetrated by Black people against white people were picked up by the Ku Klux Klan in the South, while in Maine, the Klan targeted foreigners. It had been said that as Maine elections went, so went the country, and the Klan sought political power in Maine.

Union veterans attending the GAR (Grand Army of the Republic) encampment at the former Camp Knox training grounds at the top of Talbot Avenue, 1895. *Rockland Historical Society.*

There was pushback beginning in 1920, when a chapter of the NAACP in Bangor protested the showing of *The Birth of a Nation*. A local theater owner edited out the scene at the end where the Klan gathers in white sheets and masks and burns crosses.

The chief recruiter for the Klan in Maine was F. Eugene Farnsworth, a former magician and hypnotist. Farnsworth proclaimed in the July 7, 1923 *Rockland Courier-Gazette*, "This is not an Italian nation, this is not an Irish nation, and this is not a Catholic nation, it has always been and will always be a Protestant nation." Many paid the ten-dollar membership fee and were inducted into the secret society.

"There was no lynching or violence, it was more like a social club," states Mark Alan Leslie, author of *The Crossing*, which tells a story of the Ku Klux Klan's impact on a village in western Maine. As improbable as it sounds given that Mainers helped so many slaves escape to freedom in the 1860s, in the 1920s, the Ku Klux Klan reached such influence that it helped elect Governor Ralph Owen Brewster; the mayors of Rockland, Bath, Saco and Westbrook; and many other public officials.

Flaming crosses were dramatically evil, curiously borrowed, like the hooded costumes worn by Klansmen in D.W. Griffith's film. On Christmas Eve 1923, Klansmen from Camden burned a thirty-foot-high cross at the summit of Mount Battie, and in March 1924, not to be outdone, the Rockland Klan burned a fifty-foot cross on Middle Street Hill.

Reverend E.V. Allen of Rockland was elevated to the office of grand klaliff, Realm of Maine, and in August 1924, the Klan sponsored a rally on Rockland's Middle Street Hill. Flyers let people know to gather at 10:00 p.m. It was like a party. Hundreds of automobiles parked on the old Civil War campground of Maine's Fourth Regiment between Middle and Rankin Streets. In the field opposite, vendors sold hot dogs and lemonade. After a speech, new members were "naturalized," and Klan members ignited three crosses as the crowd dispersed. After that time, the Klan continued its meetings and marched in some parades, but it had lost its cachet among the people of Maine by 1930.

The novelty of the hate group wore off. High-ranking Klansmen, including Farnsworth, were indicted for embezzlement and bribery. Although 20 percent of the state's population had joined in 1924, by 1928, the membership was fewer than one thousand. In 1934, the Klan house at 22 Brewster Street was sold.

Chapter 22

Homecoming

Louise Nevelson, in her colorful draped silks and velvets, headwrap and false fur eyelashes, was a recognizable artist in Greenwich Village, where for many years she had her studio at 29 Spring Street. Nevelson had the common trajectory of a famous artist, selling very little and receiving little appreciation until the art world caught up with her. Money from her brother and sister sometimes was what kept her going, and she was liable to spend their gifts on art supplies instead of food. Nate would come to New York with money from Louise's parents to buy her a dress, but she would tell him to forget the dress, and they would go out for a drink. Yet she became one of the most famous artists of her generation. In her prime at eighty, she returned to Rockland with an exhibition of fifty of her drawings and sculptures at the Farnsworth Museum, borrowed from the Museum of Modern Art, the Whitney Museum and private collections. The honors included receiving a key to the city.

She was born Leah Berliawsky in Kiev, Ukraine, to Mina Sadie and Isaac Berliawsky. Her father was a contractor and lumber merchant who immigrated to the United States in 1902; his wife, Louise's older brother Nathan and younger sister Lillian followed him later.

The sculptor burned with ambition from childhood. She was nine when she looked at a larger-than-life white plaster statue of Joan of Arc at the Rockland Public Library and had an epiphany that she would be an artist. "From the very beginning in my blueprint," she stated, "I projected all

Louise Nevelson in her New York studio. *Art Resource.*

this, so there are no surprises. I feel I have fulfilled my destiny." And she did recall some fond memories. She used to visit the library, and the librarian asked her what she wanted to be when she grew up. "An artist," she said promptly, but then corrected herself. "No—a sculptor; I don't want color to help me." She was tall and pretty. According to biographer Laurie Lisle, when the writer Sholem Aleichem came to America as a celebrity in 1916, he remarked to Mina that her daughter was destined for greatness, which the mother repeated.

Louise chose the library as the site of an artwork she was giving Rockland. As she generally used found objects in her work, the townspeople gathered pieces of wood to contribute to her assemblances.

Eager to move beyond a small town, she accepted the proposal of marriage of Charles Nevelson, a New York shipping broker, when she was twenty-one. She reveled in her new life in New York City; she studied modern dance, voice and art at the Art Students League and plunged into art. Meanwhile, she flouted her husband's request for her to be home by 7:00 p.m., resisting a domestic pattern. In 1922, she had a child, Myron "Mike." In 1931, she separated from her husband. Her son was sent to her parents in Rockland while Louise went off to Germany, where she worked as a film extra in Vienna and Berlin. In the 1930s, Nevelson began to create cubist abstract sculptures. She met Frida Kahlo and worked with Diego Rivera on his murals. She also worked with the Federal Arts Project (WPA). In the 1950s, she developed her monochrome assemblages, scavenging bits of discarded wood from the streets, stacking them to form walls and boxes and painting them black or another single color. Her prestige grew with sales to the Whitney and Brooklyn Museums and the Museum of Modern Art. In 1959, she exhibited a groundbreaking room-size all-white *Dawn's Wedding Feast* series at the MOMA, an abstraction representing a wedding with the bride and groom, their guests and so forth. Many of her works were intended to be installed outdoors. Outdoor sculpture is wonderful because it is public; my children grew up with Nevelson's outdoor steel sculpture in front of the Princeton Art Museum.

Louise's brother and sister graduated from Rockland High. Nate Berliawsky was a longtime popular owner of Rockland's Thorndike Hotel on Main Street. He and Lillian and her husband, Ben Mildwoff, made gifts to major museums. Nevelson's parents, who raised Mike, had a home at 4 Linden Street. He would also become an artist and live in the house of his grandparents for the rest of his life. It was said that, fierce about her art, Louise Nevelson did not mellow as a human being.

Chapter 23

Trolley

She wears a lacy shirtwaist tucked into a gabardine skirt; the matching suit jacket has fashionable leg-of-mutton sleeves. He has on a brown wool suit and a bow tie. Her hat is straw with a black silk band, and he wears a stiff bowler. Their son will take the buggy home to the farm after driving his parents to the trolley. They are off to a vaudeville show and dinner in a seaside pavilion if the weather holds.

Where are they—Brooklyn? The Hamptons? The odd truth is that they would have been catching the trolley (Rockland, Thomaston and Camden Street Railway). Manchester Haynes and George Macomber, both of Augusta and both early promoters of trolleys, acquired the Rockland, Thomaston and Camden franchise for the trolley line that the legislature had chartered. A summary of the trolley is provided by the 2009 book *Where the Mountains Meet the Sea: A History of the Camden Area 1900–2000* by Philip Conkling:

> *Although Camden and Rockport were separated politically in 1891, the towns were still closely connected. They shared business interests and skilled labor force, in the shipbuilding, lime and ice industries in particular, but they were also literally connected by the Rockland, Thomaston and Camden Street Railway, or trolley system for almost 40 years, from 1892 to 1931.*

The trolley took passengers from Camden through Rockport and Rockland to Thomaston every half hour and every hour to Warren, largely along what

The trolley. *Rockland Historical Society*.

is now Route 1. Spurs went west from downtown Rockland through the present-day intersection of Maverick and Old County Road, as well as to a resort hotel at Owls Head. Outdoor shelters were located along the line for waiting passengers, with twenty-person-capacity stations in Thomaston Village and at the Thomaston Green. According to Charlie Merrill, who made a study of the trolley, "When the line was short, the fare was five cents. As they added sections, it cost more to go a greater distance. But the shorter route probably still cost five cents." Service was quite rapid—twenty-three minutes from Thomaston to Rockland—and a trip the full length of the line from Camden to Warren would take an hour and twenty-five minutes. (Smoking was allowed only in the three rear seats.)

The trolley company had something for everybody. It ran spur lines to the lime quarries, which also ran the Lime Rock Railroad until 1942. The company's increasingly powerful generators on Powerhouse Hill in Rockport provided street lighting in Rockland and electricity for residential use in Camden and Rockport until after 1920, when the Central Maine Power Company acquired the trolley company and its electric lines.

To generate additional interest in and revenue for the passenger side of the trolley business, the company operated Oakland Park, an entertainment venue with a casino and bandbox that showed motion pictures for free. Its sprawling seventy-two-acre site, north of Glen Cove, included a baseball diamond, croquet lawns, a bandstand, a speakers' platform and facilities for fishing, swimming, dancing and ice-skating in the winter.

Twice there were serious accidents. On August 12, 1911, two cars collided, one on regular service and the other running as a special, carrying a party of schoolchildren back to Warren after a day at Oakland Park. One person was killed and six injured. The second mishap took place on January 10, 1920, at the curve near the present Rockport Opera House. The trolley car, en route to Rockland from Camden, hit the curve (on a downhill grade at a right angle) at such speed that the body of the car left the tracks and rolled over onto the ground, killing the motorman and a woman passenger and injuring nine others. Insurance claims were made, and one passenger received $5,000. The car was never used again.

The local people depended on the trolley when they did not have horses and before they all had automobiles. Its closure coincided with the onset of the Great Depression in 1931.

Today, remnants of the trolley can be found in a half dozen places, and the trolley rail bed can be viewed and walked from Warren village and from the Trolley Marsh Preserve trail. Remains of two bridges crossing tributaries of the St. George River can be visited by canoe.

The trolley's head lamp and signal bell can be seen at the Warren Historical Society.

Trolley timetables, a brochure covering the features of the trolley line and a handful of trolley tokens are available at the Walsh History Center in Camden and at the Rockland Historical Society.

Trolley cars no. 32 and 34 were sold in 1931 and became Tom's Diner in Sanford, Maine.

Chapter 24

Walter Piston

Walter Piston was a celebrated twentieth-century Italian American composer, born at 15 Ocean Street in Rockland's South End in 1894. His father, Walter Piston Sr., was a bookkeeper and his mother, Leona Stover, a local girl; a better job took the family to Boston when Walter Jr. was eleven. The composer's paternal grandfather was a sailor from Genoa, Italy, who changed his name from Antonio Pistone to Anthony Piston when he came to Maine.

Walter Piston was not a studio musician; instead, he was largely self-taught. During the 1910s, he played piano and violin in dance bands and an orchestra. Realizing he was going to be drafted in the First World War, he taught himself to play saxophone so as to join the U.S. Navy as a musician. He emerged from three years in the navy band able to play many wind instruments and continued to familiarize himself with an array of other instruments.

He went to Harvard as an older student, graduated summa cum laude and won a scholarship to study at the École Nationale de Musique in Paris. It must have been a revelation for him, as Paris was the center for new music of his day. As a consequence of studying under such great musicians as Nadia Boulanger and Paul Dukas, he led a musical style that straddled the traditional and the new.

Piston held the idea that his work had story lines or scenes. He felt he was creating impressions that balanced expression and formal design. There are melodies that come and go, and atonality that is listenable and pretty, due to his mastery of contrapuntal exchanges and orchestral timbre. Several specific

Composer Walter Piston. *Rockland Historical Society.*

works are atmospheric reflections of the Maine coast. The effect is of the changing surface of the ocean; the composer spoke of the "controlled expansion and development of two or three short musical motives."

A man approached him after going to the premiere of his *Three New England Sketches* (1959) and said, "I hope you don't mind my saying that I smelled clams during the first movement." Piston replied, "No, that is quite all right. They are your clams." The first of these sketches is "Seaside (Adagio)." It is imbued with the shore and sky. Faintly, the waves are heard in light, life-like percussion. The weather darkens. At the end, it is as though the tide has gone out and little shore creatures are returning. A late piece was "Pine Tree Fantasy" (1965). In his music, there are primary and secondary melodies, and he exulted in changing meters and tunes carried by different instruments to pay homage to anything from a dance-hall waltz to country fiddling.

As a Harvard professor from 1926 until his retirement in 1960, Piston was a much-loved person and wrote significant textbooks to teach others about the piano and composition. Among his many students were Elliott Carter, Leroy Anderson and Leonard Bernstein. Among his rewards were three New York Music Critics' Circle Awards for a viola concerto and a string quartet, two Pulitzer Prizes and eight honorary doctorates. He composed a ballet suite, *The Incredible Flutist*, which premiered at the Boston Pops and has entered our general musical culture as a familiar work (especially the sensual "Tango of the Merchant's Daughter" early in the ballet). This is music of utmost joy and verve. A live 2015 performance from Madrid's Teatro Monumental can be heard on the Internet.

Armand Pohan, the president of NY Waterway, the ferry fleet in the harbor of New York, is also a concert pianist whom I first heard perform at my older brother's graduation from the Englewood School for Boys in New Jersey. He recalled:

> *During my years at Harvard I heard quite a number of his works. Piston was a professor in the Harvard Music Department whose textbooks on*

counterpoint and orchestration are still considered definitive. He would therefore have taught every music major who attended Harvard from 1926 to 1960, including Bernstein, Elliott Carter and Leroy Anderson. The Boston Symphony Orchestra was the usual venue for the premiere of any of his orchestral works, and so he could often be heard on the radio, either live or in recordings. The first concert I ever heard at Sanders Theatre—actually the first live orchestral concert I ever attended—included his Three New England Sketches, *with Charles Munch conducting. Piston was in the audience and came onstage to take a bow.*

I've never heard the Three New England Sketches *since that night, although I remember liking it—if not as much as Charles Ives's atmospheric and haunting* Three Places in New England. *In the context of his musical era, I would consider Piston to be a conservative composer, still writing symphonies with tonal centers at a time when his American contemporaries were either writing twelve-tone music like Carter or Babbitt (Piston did increasingly experiment with this toward the end of his life) or works outside of the usual classical forms which draw upon jazz, folk or faux-folk melody, e.g., Bernstein, Copland, Dello Joio. One exception would be Piston's (only) ballet,* The Incredible Flutist, *a very lively and colorful work which includes a circus scene with a barking dog. My recollection is that Piston's works are usually very rhythmically interesting and very well-orchestrated.*

The birthplace of the composer still stands on Ocean Street.

Chapter 25

Andre's Odyssey

One cove up from the busy commercial Rockland Harbor is Rockport Harbor. For decades, people made pilgrimages there from April to October to watch the show provided by Harry Goodridge, the Rockport harbormaster, and Andre, his pet harbor seal. Andre had been rescued as a pup from the Penobscot Bay and became adjusted to living in the Goodridge family's house, as well as outdoors on their property. Harry had already trained a robin, a pigeon, a seagull and a bat.

Andre became one of the family. He went scuba diving with Harry and was incorrigible about playing around the boats in the harbor. He went sledding and on car trips with the family, splashed around in their bathtub and learned to watch TV and shake hands.

This playful and devoted seal showed up in Rockport Harbor during summers to be with his human friends. He wintered in the Boston or Mystic Aquarium. Released each spring, he made his way 150 miles back to Rockport. Andre kept up this pattern for twenty-five years. He spent his last days in the Rockport Harbor and had to be helped up from the water to the harbormaster's house by four strong men.

Did the Greek hero Odysseus manage to return home because of his extraordinary seamanship, or did the gods make it happen? Was Andre's navigational feat innate in his species of marine mammal? Was the capacity for friendship with people singular to one stand-out seal?

A partial answer has been emerging from a scientific study showing that harbor seals can pilot, or "steeplechase," by moving from landmark to

Andre in his pen. *Penobscot Marine Museum.*

landmark. In 2008, one Danish and two German biologists published results of the first evidence for star orientation capability in a marine mammal in a study of two harbor seals orienting in a custom-made floating planetarium. Both seals learned to accurately identify a lodestar out of a random projection of the Northern Hemisphere night system.

The experimental setting involved a planetarium dome built on a ring of pontoons over which the realistic six thousand nighttime stars were projected. First, the seals were guided with a handheld laser pointer to the lodestars' azimuth position, and they learned to indicate this position when the laser pointed to the lodestar. After abandoning the laser pointer and leaving one of the seals alone in the planetarium, it was found that each seal gradually increased the accuracy of its performance to 100 percent correct choices. The study suggests that seals can steer by the stars when traveling in open seas, or, as the scientists concluded, "Visual pattern recognition and identity concept formation capability of seals can certainly be assumed to be sufficiently efficient to identify lodestars within salient star constellations of the night sky."

Andre and Harry put on free shows in Rockport every day from April to late fall. Come late fall, Harry would take Andre in his station wagon to a safe harbor in Massachusetts or Connecticut. He would guide him to the edge of the water, so in this way, the seal spent some winters at the New England Aquarium in Boston and others at the Mystic Aquarium in Mystic, Connecticut. But Andre always swam back to see Harry when released in the spring. Sometimes he did special appearances. Harry watched to be sure Andre wasn't made uncomfortable by being asked to do tricks but said he loved the attention. He lived an unusually long life of twenty-five years, perhaps not wanting to disappoint his friends. He couldn't jump through a hoop when his eyesight failed, but he could still shoot baskets.

According to Professor Les Kaufman of Boston University, harbor seals do migrate seasonally, like many other large marine species.

How do the seals navigate? Dr. Jelle Atema, professor emeritus of Boston University and formerly of the Woods Hole Oceanographic Institute, observed:

> *Given the large scale of the trip it is most likely that seals use a sun compass and a magnetic compass. An additional sense might be flow and wave detection. These senses are known, but how they work is still under intense debate. Typically, you can assume other senses playing a role when they arrive in the general area, which they may remember visually from a previous visit or by odor or sound.*

But also remarkable was the bond of affection that impelled Andre to use his innate compasses to make an extreme journey home by himself, year after year, passing through waters where there are very few seals, beginning when he was a curious pup and swam to Harry's boat in May 1961.

Dr. Atema continued:

> *Consider that the wild seal resembles a domesticated dog. There are many stories about dogs (and cats) who relocate their earlier residence after the family moves…sometimes over very large distances, comparable to the Gulf of Maine for Andre. Andre was rescued (and tamed) by a human. Perhaps*

The seal Andre, Rockport. *Nasser K.*

> *Andre is like a rescued dog who kisses the new owner (licks the human face) just as Andre seems to do in one of the published pictures. Both dogs and maybe seals are strongly bonded and take risks to reunite. The big difference is that the domesticated dog does not have to migrate.*

Harborside in Rockport, a fine granite statue depicts Andre. Many visit this beautiful out-of-the-way spot to pay homage to an intelligent and loving creature that became a legend of the Mid-Coast.

Chapter 26

COMEBACK

Rockland is an active seaport with a huge harbor in the midst of the best cruising grounds of Maine at the mouth of the Penobscot Bay. Combining maritime industry, yachting, boat building, ferry and bus service, the bustling harbor is located a short walk from the attractions of dining, shopping, museums and art galleries on Main Street. Its Lobster Festival every summer celebrates the city. Off-season it is vibrant too, and the colored lights on its gigantic lobster trap Christmas tree celebrate its distinction of being the Lobster Capital of the World.

Landmark federal legislation, the Clean Air Act of 1970 and the Clean Water Act of 1972, began a reversal that significantly improved the harbor's water quality over the next two decades. The last big fish plant, located on the north end of the waterfront below Maverick Street, was bought by a Texas-based energy company, Zapata, in the early 1980s but closed its doors when Zapata failed in its efforts to minimize escalating complaints about smell. The end of the fish packing business was the turning point of Rockland's renascence. The grease on the water that boats encountered entering the harbor disappeared, and the harbor and its docks became a sparkling transportation hub by sea and by land.

Part of the revitalization is credited to full-time harbormasters Ken M. Rich and his successor, Ed Glazer. "Harbormaster" has the ring of long ago but is a critical feature of coastal U.S. cities. There are currently 650 boat moorings, four marinas, eight commercial windjammers and a half-dozen sailing vessels and powerboats conducting day trips.

Rock City Cafe. *Aidan Kaczynski.*

In 2010, the National Trust for Historic Preservation named Rockland as one of a dozen "distinctive destinations." Once a stepchild of Camden, Rockland was soon hailed for its thriving downtown and as Maine's center for the arts, with fine galleries, the Farnsworth Museum, the Center for Maine Contemporary Art and summer classes that draw artists from across the nation. Arguably the heroine of the comeback lived two centuries earlier—Lucy Farnsworth, the cultivated, reclusive and determined woman who was the major benefactor of the Farnsworth Art Museum. Lucy dreamed of a great art museum in her hometown, and this has become the city of Rockland's greatest treasure.

Chapter 27

The Strand

Rockland already had two theaters when the Strand opened in 1923 with the silent movie *My Wild Irish Rose*. The excitement about this one was that it showed silent movies, with live music performed on a pipe organ. The Strand is a building that has a living past, and its story starts with a Russian Jew in the grocery business named Joe Dondis. A 1920 fire destroyed a whole block, and Joe's wife, Ida, suggested that another stable wasn't needed now that there were automobiles. Over the winter of 1922, the new theater was built by local labor, with horse-drawn sleds pulling the bricks. The theater was state of the art, and although it was a movie theater, it was constructed so space could be added for vaudeville.

Small in person but immense in character, Dondis stood up to the competing interests in film distribution and once sued Paramount to get a fair deal. When he died, Ida ran the theater for another forty-five years, and their son Meredith carried on the tradition until 2001. It served the community with a panoply of entertainment, but the premises were aging. When the Flagship chain bought the Strand, they closed it down to eliminate a competitor to their Thomaston multiplex. The grand old movie house was boarded up. The tides turned because a *Rockland Courier-Gazette* reporter brought to the attention of the Maine attorney general what had happened, and the Flagship corporation was instructed to resell within ninety days to someone intending to operate the Strand as a theater.

The Strand had fans, one of whom was Matthew Simmons, a Houston-based energy banker who came to Rockland every summer and liked to bring

Strand Theater. *Nasser K.*

his family on a rainy Saturday to the Strand. Because he loved old movies and theaters and had admired a renovated Deco theater in Savannah, he made a flat offer and bought the theater in 2003. After a complete renovation, it reopened in 2005 as a venue for musical and dramatic performances, lectures and films. "The way I might collect nickels, Simmons collected old buildings," said the Strand's current manager, Liz McLeod. "Matthew Simmons collected old buildings. And he hired John Fry, the contractor who had done a reconstruction on his house, to renovate the theater. He was one of the most down-to-earth wealthy people. He carried no airs....He had a vision of a theater for everyone, not just high end. We have a strong base in the community."

The renovation took eighteen months. Bringing the Strand back to its 1920s glamour meant reupholstering and repainting the 1968 seats and adding new carpeting, a new tin ceiling and all new bricks to replace the badly deteriorated ones.

The change to nonprofit status was part of a lengthy process that began following the benefactor's death in 2010 and was completed in 2013, when Mrs. Simmons donated the physical property of the building to the newly formed Friends of the Strand Theater. The original board of the nonprofit organization was chaired by Jo Dondis, Joseph and Ida Dondis's granddaughter. The Friends assumed full responsibility for the Strand in 2013 and have operated on a nonprofit basis ever since.

Among the Strand's offerings are independent films, vintage films and classics, operas from the Metropolitan in high-definition, National Theater of London productions and Bolshoi ballets, live concerts, family presentations, live stage shows and a live radio show. "If someone comes with an interesting show, we figure out how to do it," stated McLeod. "We've had a trained eagle act and Victorian magic lantern show and great indie movies. We spent years upgrading the ventilation system. We added acoustical panels and state-of-the-art restrooms and lobbies on two floors. But we want to make it feel as it always has because people here like familiarity."

Chapter 28

Dick Spear

It was the theoretical perspective of the greatest historian of his day, Samuel Eliot Morison, that the most significant arenas of the relations of the United States with the rest of the world were on the seas. He co-wrote an eloquent textbook during his forty years teaching at Harvard University that put forth his view. His studies took him all the way back to 1492 and led to his quest to retrace the voyages of Columbus and determine how good a sea captain he really was.

With three hundred books and many ancient charts and logs, this expedition—first in the barkentine *Capitana*, named after one of Columbus's larger ships, departing Connecticut for the Azores and Lisbon and then switching to a smaller sailing vessel, the forty-five-foot ketch *Mary Otis* (the size of the *Niña*)—retraced Columbus's route from Europe to Cuba by way of Cádiz, Madeira and the Canary Islands. Instead of selecting one of his Harvard students to be a mate, Morison chose a Rockland High School student, Richard "Dick" G. Spear, son of an adult member of the crew.

Morison's *Admiral of the Ocean Sea* recounted the results of the expedition through ports and waters of Europe, Africa, South America and the Caribbean. It won a Pulitzer Prize in 1943, but Professor Morison's claim to have proved that Columbus went ashore in San Salvador has remained controversial. A recent discovery of a 1500 map by the master of the *Santa Maria* suggests a different island for Columbus's landfall. All the same, Morison's expedition was an imaginative plan carried out with gusto. An academic, he threw himself into his impressive quest, and clearly it was

Above: Construction crew of nineteen men and a boy at a shipyard wharf in Rockland shortly after the 1913 launch of a schooner. *Penobscot Marine Museum.*

Right: *Captain Richard G. Spear* ferry, launched in 2021. *Maine Department of Transportation.*

a great adventure for all. Dick was the youngest member of the team at seventeen, about the age when Columbus, trained as a weaver, probably went to sea in the late 1460s. Dick's picture appeared on the front cover of *Life* magazine in 1940, months before the Japanese attack on Pearl Harbor.

A newly minted midshipman and a Mainer, my dad was aboard a ship that sank at Pearl Harbor. What struck me when I read a feature in the local Rockland newspaper about Dick Spear was the similarity between the two men. The *Rockland Courier-Gazette* captioned the photo: "R.G. Spear, better known to the world as 'Dick,' wears a sober cast of countenance, but inwardly he is all thrills." A parallel remark was in my father's Naval Academy yearbook, that he was a sober, serious person but given the nickname "Giggles."

Spear graduated from the second class of the Maine Maritime Academy and embarked on a sixty-year maritime career. During World War II, he served in war zones around the globe. After the war, he rose to be the first ferry master of the Maine State Ferry Service, a position he held until his retirement in 1980. He had a pilot's license and journeyed in his plane and on land from the Arctic to Antarctica. The new ferry built in East Boothbay for the Rockland-Vinalhaven route is named *Captain Richard G. Spear*.

PART II

ST. GEORGE PENINSULA

Chapter 1

Introduction

Five boroughs may make up New York City, but St. George comprises nine villages and fifty-three islands. Here is a list of villages, based on the criterion of having a post office now or formerly: Clark Island (1884–1961); Elmore (1901–1923), also known as Harts Neck; Glenmere (1892–1942); Long Cove; Martinsville (1878–1918); Port Clyde (known as South St. George from 1829 to 1880, when the name was changed to Port Clyde); St. George (1828–1993); Spruce Head (1880–present); and Tenants Harbor (1852–present). Burnt Island is the locus of camping for Hurricane Island Outward Bound School. The Brothers (three islands) are a Nature Conservancy bird rookery. In 2022, Colby College became the steward of Allen and Benner Islands. The peninsula's beautiful town forest is Kinney Woods.

Eva worked her whole life; usually, that meant several jobs. She packed fish and shrimp and worked at the sardine factory and for the Port Clyde water distribution company. Between times, she picked crabmeat. For many years, she worked in the general store, usually opening at seven o'clock and in the winter closing too: "I knew everybody, often including the summer people. The owner would shake his head and ask me, 'Who are these people?'"

The Cushmans are well known and influential in the fishing industry. Altogether, Eva and her husband, a lobsterman, raised seven children, the first four in the first five years of marriage. "The older ones watched the younger ones, and my husband, on days he didn't haul, tended the kids."

Above: Tenants Harbor. *Nasser K.*

Opposite: Fisherman and his wife dolls by the Port Clyde Baptist Church Circle. *Nasser K.*

She holds her head proudly. "It always seemed to take two of us to pay the bills." There are sixty-nine of the Cushman family in the line of Eva and her descendants, "with two more coming." Many of them, including three of her daughters and their families, are close by. They rotate every day to see what she needs help with, and so she knows whose favorite pie to make for Sunday dinner. She is the center of the machinery of a big happy family of which she is the eldest member. With conviction she said, "I like my independence. I never went looking."

When the boats came in, Eva and her children would go down the hill and watch them unload. Her husband went out every day in good weather.

Weather was life's critical factor. One February, one of her sons didn't come home in a snowstorm and was found drowned at Burnt Island.

When Eva retired, she still made donuts for the general store and took a part-time job in billing for the water company, but she still had time on her hands, so she joined the Baptist church sewing circle. This legendary group of local women sewed, knitted and quilted for the church. Beginning in the late '70s, for two decades she made dolls, about nine hundred in total. She made clothes for her family, pants for the boys and knitted and crocheted: "I learned crochet from my grandma and picked up knitting myself, because I am left-handed and figured out how to knit like right-handed folks." She knitted nylon-mesh pot heads for lobster traps too. "I knit my husband an Irish sweater he only wore once and gave it to the girls. Then I knit him a crewneck navy sweater. He thanked me, but I was in the fish house once and saw it hanging on a nail. I knit socks and more socks for everybody. My husband did wear the wristers and mittens I knit, but he was all khaki; now fishermen wear anything."

The Baptist church fair was known far and wide, and Eva knitted many garments and made many dolls for it. Customers lined up before it opened. At 6:30 a.m., there were people waiting, so Greg Mott's wife baked muffins and coffee for the people in line.

In her mid-nineties, Eva could mesmerize anybody with her storytelling. Did you know that after a certain shipwreck, heritage turnip seeds were

Above: A boatful of dolls at Eva Cushman's house in Port Clyde. *Nasser K.*

Left: Eva Cushman with the author. *Nasser K.*

Opposite: Port Clyde fisherfolk: Eva's grandson Randy Cushman, son of Lee, who also operated a dragger. Randy's brothers Mike, Gerry and Dennis are lobstermen. *Kathleen Fox.*

recovered and sown? She does admit to missing sitting on her porch that is now artist Barbara Prey's gallery after work at the factory and seeing people who would wave and chat. She pointed out favorite quilts in her home: "That one was delivered with my soup, a gift from the minister's wife. She is colorblind, as you can guess, and she used a big mix of colors and fabrics, but it came out so nice."

Eva is the custodian of a group of unsold dolls. "I made the big fisherman doll," she said. "I kept a list of the people from all over who bought our dolls. I have cut out a few more, but after making six hundred of them, I can hardly look at the fabrics."

Chapter 2

Early Encounter

Historic sources about the several eras of Native people on the Maine coast are scanty. Even the impression of the seasonality of the Wabanakis in Maine—by which they planted their corn and beans at the shore in, say, April, fished and hunted along the coast for the summer and withdrew into the deep woods after the harvest—are incomplete, as likely they went into the woods because they were wary of the Europeans on their shores. There are both documents and mysteries concerning the first contact of European colonizers with the Indigenous people of Maine.

George Weymouth, the first sea captain to go up the St. George River, had an amanuensis, as Samuel Johnson had James Boswell. Ferdinand Gorges, a soldier and the governor of Portsmouth (England), equipped the *Archangell* and sent Weymouth with a crew of twenty-six on an exploratory mission. Gorges (an English aristocrat with a non–English sounding name) had a vision of ruling prosperous settlements in northern New England. James Rosier went along on the *Archangell* to report and glamorize. Rosier was an enlightened person who reminds me of Dr. Maturin, the ship's surgeon in the Patrick O'Brian sea novels. The account published shortly after the vessel's return to England was literary and enthusiastic. It told how the expedition anchored at what is now Allen Island and planted a garden there—the first agricultural foray of Europeans in North America. It had details about the Native people as well as about spring in New England that were scientific, if hyperbolic. For instance, when Rosier raved about the

Scrawl of a crew member of the *Archangell*, 1605. Nasser K.

St. George River as "the most rich, beautiful, large & secure harbouring river that the world afforteth," he cited crew members who had traveled on the Oronoco, the Seine and the Thames. The Native people's "excellent ingenious" birchbark canoes and rich beaver skin mantles were described. Rosier's narrative, *A True Relation of the Most Prosperous Voyage Made This Present Year, 1605, by Captain George Weymouth in the Discovery of the North Part of Virginia*, is a precious document about the encounter of the Europeans and the inhabitants.

The *Archangell* had departed England on March 31, 1605, and was exploring Monhegan and Allen Islands in May. A launch, a workboat assembled on the *Archangell* (it could be sailed or rowed), went up the St.

George River on June 11 while a few crew members rowed ashore on the Meduncook River (which is separated from the St. George River by the Cushing Peninsula, i.e., Gay Island and Pleasant Point). Thomas King, the bosun, was among those waiting for the return of the launch, and he whiled away his time by incising the ledge along the riverbank. This scrawl, "Thos. King," with the date 1605 and a cross (mimetic of the cross Weymouth set up on Allen Island on May 29), although faint, remains. Few had seen it or believed in the veracity until a young man brought the inscription to the attention of the Maine Historic Preservation Commission. This led to its authentication, and in 1978, the site was placed in the National Register of Historic Places. The *Archangell* would return to England in July of the same year, anchoring in Dartmouth.

By happy circumstance, the bosun was singled out in Rosier's account for being an excellent fisherman:

> *Wherefore our sailes being downe, Thomas King boatswaine, presently cast out a hook, and before he judged it at ground, was fished and haled up an exceeding great and well fed Cod, then there were cast out 3 or 4 more, and the fish was so plentiful and so great. As when our Captaine would have set sail, we all desired him to suffer them to take fish a while.*

Also from Rosier's account:

> *Thursday, 30 May, 1605*
> *This day, about 5.00 o'clock in the afternoon we in the shippe espied three canoas coming toward us which went to the island adjoining us where they went ashore and very quickly had a fire about which they stood regarding our ship.—they sent one canoa with three men to our ship—to these we gave such things as we saw they liked.*
>
> *The shape of their body is very proportionable, they are well countenanced not very tall nor big, but in stature like us.*
>
> *They paint their bodies with black, their faces some with red, some black and some with blew.*
>
> *Their clothing is beavers skins, or Deare skins, cast over them like a mantle and hanging down to their knees, made fast together upon the shoulders with leather; some of them had sleeves, most had none. Some had buskins of such leather sewed; they have beside a piece of Beaver skin between their legs.*

> *They suffer no hair to grow on their faces but on their head very long and very black, which those that have wives, bind up behind with a leather string in a long round knot.*
>
> *We found them all very civill and merrie—we found them of exceedingly good intention, quick understanding and ready capacity.*
>
> *Their Canoas are made without iron of the bark of a birch tree, strengthened within with ribs and hoops of wood, in so good fashion with such excellent ingenius art, as they are able to bear seven or eight persons.*
>
> *The next morning three Salvages came in a canoa, we enticed them below deck and fed them pork, fish, bread and pease, all of which they did eat. I noted that they would eat nothing raw, either fish or flesh.*
>
> *I saw their bows and arrows, which I took up and drew an arrow in one of them, which I found to be of strength able to carry an arrow five or six score strong. Their bow is made of Witch Hazell and some of Beech, in fashion much like ours. But they want nocks, only a string of leather put through a hole in one end and made fast with a knot at the other.*
>
> *Their arrows are made of the same wood, some of ash, big and long, with three feathers tied on and nocked very artificially, headed with the long shank bone of a Deere, made very sharp with two fangs in the manner of a harping iron.*
>
> *They have likewise darts, headed with bone, one of which I darted among the rocks and it brake not.*

Somehow, the picture of an Englishman contemporary of William Shakespeare skipping an arrowhead across the rocks of the St. George River is boggling. Indeed, one of the backers of the expedition was Henry Wriothesley, Third Earl of Southampton, to whom Shakespeare dedicated his two narrative poems, *Venus and Adonis* and *The Rape of Lucretia.*

The ledge where King wrote his inscription is sedimentary rock built up over eons, which was then turned from its original horizontal orientation to nearly vertical by geologic movements. The striking ridges of white and gray seen in the bedrock are actually the layers of sediment—softer than granite—which is why King could carve in it (and why it is eroding). What's more, the tide line is shifting slowly from when the exceptionally keen young man "from away" discovered it in 1979. One day it may not be above the tide line. However, the graceful writing itself and the open view of the sea and Allen Island from the ledge provided me with as moving an experience of a historical landmark as I have had anywhere in the world.

Location of the scrawl on the rock ledge. *Nasser K.*

Unfortunately, the mood of exploration and friendly encounter soon darkened. The English went to dinner at the Native American camp but came away uneasy, as there were many who appeared to be warriors. Thus, Captain Weymouth reciprocated with a dinner on his boat and invited his guests to sleep below deck. They did, and three seem to have been forced to stay. Rosier and half a dozen others went ashore, ostensibly to trade and eat peas around the campfire. The Englishmen grabbed two more of the Wabanaki "savages" by their long hair. Unashamed of the treachery—the colonizers viewed their society as superior to all others—Weymouth sailed up the river. He had already put a cross on Allen Island and now erected another near the present site of Thomaston and then returned to the mouth of the river and took soundings. With his kidnapped prizes and after more enthusiastic sightseeing, he sailed back to England. The ambitions of Ferdinand Gorges grew when Captain Weymouth brought him three captive men of the Wabanaki tribe; he sponsored another venture that bankrupted him. But King James I called the guests to court and was impressed by them. The captives were polite and learned English but longed for home, and several, as soon as they could, returned to Maine. Two of the Wabanaki were taken on a re-survey expedition that ended up in the West Indies. The "scouts" spent several years in a Spanish prison, and one is recorded as being back eventually in Gorges's household. Another sailed with Martin Pring on the Jamestown Expedition and made it home to Mid-Coast Maine.

When the Pilgrims began their colony, a visitor came out of the woods of Plymouth and said, "Welcome, English." This was Samoset, who introduced a friend or ally, Squanto (Tisquantum), to the Pilgrims. Squanto may have been one of the five Wabanakis who had sailed off in the *Archangell* fifteen years earlier.

Chapter 3
Deeds

Long ago, the Thomaston side of the Georges River belonged to the English and the peninsula side to the French. However, that was very vague. Samuel Waldo of Boston owned the entire St. George Peninsula in the eighteenth century until he lost it for being a Tory in the American Revolution.

Waldo had made an agreement with the Native Americans that he would not allow settlers on the east side of the river, which functioned as a frontier between the English and the French. The north side had long been claimed by the French as part of Acadia; it was only given up when they were defeated in the 1760s in the French and Indian War. The effect of the standoff from the 1600s is that the St. George Peninsula was more or less floating free.

Waldo brought indentured Scotch-Irish and German people to his tracts, promising more than he provided the first years, but they survived and in so doing rooted his ownership. At his death, Samuel Waldo had 400,000 acres of the coastal and inland region. He died intestate, perhaps not willing to cause squabbles in his life among his heirs. While he possessed the patent, he had sold or given to relatives thousands of the original tract, in Waldoboro, Warren, Cushing (including the St. George Peninsula) and Thomaston. Samuel Waldo's son Francis went to England and sold his 2,000 acres to Alexander Wedderbourn, Earl of Roslyn, the same man who prosecuted Benjamin Franklin for anonymously publishing letters of Massachusetts governor Hutchinson to the British government in the *Boston*

Gazette in June 1773. Hutchinson had urged the British government to send more troops to Boston to suppress the American rebels. The populace of Boston was offended, Franklin was dismissed as postmaster general for the colonies and Hutchinson was called back to England.

Of Franklin's many friends in London, one was Dr. Benjamin Vaughan (1751–1835), a political economist, merchant and fellow of the Royal Society of Edinburgh, who tried to bring peace toward the end of the War of Independence. Benjamin Vaughan was also the publisher of Franklin's *Political, Miscellaneous and Philosophical Pieces.* He took pains to carry through with the project, collecting and editing, with apologies for taking "sundry liberties," the pieces he wished to include. The first sets of sheets were sent to Franklin in 1779, amid war, two and a half years after the project was started; the volume was released to the public in December 1779. The whole book ran to 550 pages.

Benjamin Vaughan's father was a banker and West India planter/merchant. Father and son were members of the America Philosophical Society in Philadelphia. Benjamin defended slavery in Jamaica in his maiden speech in Parliament in 1792, but by 1794, he spoke out in favor of abolition of the slave trade. He went back and forth between England and America until his arrest in 1794 on the grounds of treason, purportedly aiding the French to invade England. At this juncture, Benjamin and his family returned to the United States permanently, first in Boston; Jamaica Plain may have been named after him. By 1797, he was where his younger brother Charles had settled in 1791, in Hallowell, Massachusetts, an up-and-coming town with mills on the Kennebunk River. Charles's brother-in-law by his wife, Frances Apthorp, was Charles Bulfinch, the architect who changed the face of American buildings from wood to stone and created the rush to quarry granite in the Mid-Coast of Maine.

When Henry Knox died in 1806, his wife, Lucy, sold at auction lands that he had not sold off, a quarter of the 8,015 acres. Deeds were by now being carefully registered, and in 1820, Charles Vaughan was in England and obtained the land that Francis Waldo had sold. Wedderbourn (the Earl of Roslyn) transferred a third of the 8,015 acres to Charles Vaughan for the sum of one dollar. Five years later, Charles Vaughan appointed an agent named Benjamin Joy to dispose of the land in South Thomaston and St. George, which amounted to three-quarters of the 8,015-acre tract. In the sales, the land was broken into many parcels. This was the end of the great swath of lands such as the St. George Peninsula and Waldo and Knox Counties being sold intact.

When in the year before Knox's death he sold off many islands, it is recorded that one of the purchasers, Joseph Barrell, paid 800 Spanish milled dollars, worth 24 pounds lawful money, for one-half of one-twentieth of a whole share.

The plantation name for Cushing and St. George was St. Georges. When it became an incorporated town in 1789, it did so as Cushing, after the lieutenant governor of Massachusetts, Thomas Cushing. The eastern part of the town separated from the western part (that remained Cushing) in 1803 under the name of St. George. There was one more change in the town line during the Civil War, purportedly at the behest of a person living in Spruce Head, who, disturbed that citizens were slow to enlist, said he wasn't going to live in a town full of southerners. The land divisions continued. Sometimes Samuel Waldo sold property twice and sometimes someone bartered a section, like a woodlot for meadow land.

Spruce Head is an island connected to the mainland only "for a second" by a causeway; Hupper Island has four year-round and twenty-six seasonal dwellings; and Allen Island has sheep as well as two year-round and three seasonal dwellings. And of course, certain islands have evocative names, including Raspberry, Blubber, Ram, Eagle, Mosquito, Grandfather's, Spectacles, Hen, Calf and Mouse Island.

Chapter 4

Lucy Flucker Knox

Henry Knox (1750–1806) was the seventh of ten sons of upstanding Presbyterians whose fine home on what is now Federal Street overlooked Boston Harbor. His father, William, a shipbuilder and merchant from Derry, Northern Ireland, had his own wharf and import business, but when the British stopped allowing Americans to print paper money, an economic depression ensued, and the once prosperous William Knox was left destitute. William fled to St. Eustatius in the Caribbean, never to return, and Henry's mother, Mary, was obliged to take nine-year-old Henry out of the Boston Latin Grammar School. Henry, strapping, personable and smart, got employment at an upscale Boston bookshop and was able to support his mother and younger brother.

Here he was noticed by Lucy Flucker. Lucy was the maternal granddaughter of Samuel Waldo, to whom the British had given a gigantic parcel of land in what is now Maine because of his role in capturing the French fort at Louisburg in 1745 in the French and Indian War and who is remembered for bringing indentured servants to Waldoboro. Lucy found excuses to return often to the bookshop and fell in love with the handsome lad who served her. Henry and Lucy married, against her father's will (Mr. Flucker's opposition was political, as he was a Loyalist). The day after the Battle of Lexington and Concord, the young couple left Boston in a small boat. It was hard to hide Henry's identity due to his being a giant of a man. Lucy sewed his sword into her coat.

Montpelier, 1929 re-creation of the 1794 home of Henry and Lucy Knox. *Nasser K.*

In the course of the American Revolution, Henry Knox became both one the most trusted advisers of George Washington and also the minister of war. He seems to have been everywhere at once. The officer Benedict Arnold sent yard goods to Lucy in 1776 to give to a younger woman he was wooing. Seeing that his proposal was going nowhere, Lucy kept the fabric and had a dress made of it for herself.

One of Knox's stunning achievements was moving sixty tons of cannon three hundred miles on ox sleds in winter from Ticonderoga to the Dorchester Heights opposite Boston. He and Lucy hated to be separated, and besides that, they were a charming couple. Lucy met Martha Washington at dinner in Cambridge, Massachusetts, when Washington's army was encamped there. Lucy and her first baby stayed at Henry's artillery headquarters on the foot of Broadway in New York City. The couple were having breakfast when a fleet of British ships appeared in the harbor. Cannon fire began, but the British forces landed at Sandy Hook. "I scolded like a fury at her for not having gone before," Henry fumed to a friend. Soon he was leading an attack on Princeton and puncturing a portrait of George III in Nassau Hall, while Lucy spent most of the war in Boston with the children, whom she had one after the other, and at Mount Vernon for the duration of one pregnancy and the Siege of Yorktown. She wrote of how she used to sit at the window watching for Henry and how, when she saw him coming, her heart leapt for joy. Lucy could not have anticipated months of separation caused by the Revolution. She was with Knox at Valley Forge, escorted by Benedict Arnold. The relationship of the Knoxes was seen by others as an ideal complement; General Greene wrote to his wife that he found them to be a "perfect married couple."

Festive parties continued when they were together. It was the correct thing for elite women, plus Henry was gregarious and loved to entertain. When headquartered at West Point in 1782, he organized a day of festivities to celebrate the birth of the French Dauphin, the child of Louis XVI, attended by General Washington. A newspaper reported that General Washington was unusually cheerful and, with Mrs. Knox his partner, "carried down a dance of 20 couples in the arbor on the green grass." When promoted to brigadier, Knox wrote to Lucy with excitement but also conscious of the reality of war, telling her that "the man who follows [it] as such will meet with his proper demerits in another world."

Henry was given by Washington the task of overseeing the development of a U.S. Navy, which he did to his great credit. Then he retired to his dream house, in the packet of land that Lucy had inherited (including what are now Thomaston and Rockland), curiously calling it Montpelier just as James Madison's family house was called, in honor of the French assistance in the War for Independence. To impress his wife, Henry had all the materials for the most elegant house that Maine had ever seen floated up the St. George River to a beautiful prospect just before the riverbend at Thomaston. Lucy had wanted to live on their property, but she ended up heartily disliking the rural setting. A gracious hostess to famous people such as the Marquis de Lafayette's son and Talleyrand, she would not step down on the earth from her carriage or let her husband bring friends home for dinner. The mansion had dozens of bedrooms and a flying staircase; its grounds were palatial. Thomas Jefferson wrote to Knox, "Have you become a farmer? Is it not pleasanter than to be shut up within four walls and delving internally with the pen?"

Henry had boundless ideas. Even when his fortunes plummeted, he foresaw, ahead of his time, their restoration through limestone and granite. The Knox family eventually lost their wealth by Henry's financial overreach and real estate greed. A popular and revered man and good help to Washington, Knox died by choking on a chicken bone. Of Lucy and Henry's thirteen children, only three survived to outlive Lucy. She was living with her daughter Caroline, the widow of John Holmes, a U.S. senator, when she died in June 1824 at age sixty-seven, three days short of what would have been fifty years since her marriage. It was reported that in her last days, she imagined she was young again and dancing with Henry at a ball. Lucy claimed the rents from squatters who had settled on the St. George Peninsula after the Revolution, believing the land was freely theirs.

Montpelier gradually fell to ruin and was torn down in 1871 for the construction of the Knox and Lincoln Railroad. However, local people, spearheaded by Cyrus Curtis, owner of the Curtis Publishing Co., and the Daughters of the American Revolution, admiring the beauty of Montpelier and Henry Knox's outstanding part as a Patriot, joined together during the Depression to build a replica of the mansion, which opened to the public in 1930.

Either Samuel Waldo or Henry Knox may be the model for the villain of *The House of Seven Gables*, that great and beloved classic of American literature. Its author, Nathaniel Hawthorne, mentioned the chicken bone accident in his diary when visiting his friend Senator Jonathan Cilley of Thomaston.

Chapter 5

Ocean View Grange

Residents of St. George rely on their general stores in Port Clyde and Tenants Harbor but not so much for vegetables. When the sign goes up that the farmers' market at the Ocean View Grange is opening weekly, the delectable produce from local gardens is a welcome commodity rather than having to drive forty minutes to the nearest supermarket in the cold months (in my case, for the greens my pet rabbits covet). And the things they have! Interesting herbs and garlics, vinegars and oils, roots and tubers, colorful squashes, beets, potatoes and so on. The Grange at Wiley's Corner (built in 1908) is a lively place for music and discussion. Instrumentalists played one at a time one evening when I went to hear my friend the artist and coffin maker Mr. Hupper perform; many of these artists had been playing together for over fifty years.

The Grange began in 1867 as a grassroots movement. Granges have had a strong presence in Maine from their role as an adult education resource to sponsoring debates, festivals and fairs. The movement arrived in Maine by 1873. Initially, it had rituals and symbols like the Freemasons, and small ceremonial tools were once displayed. Granges had secret meetings and passwords for self-protection to keep railroad spies out of their meetings. Three years later, there were over two hundred Granges in Maine, and by 1907, the per capita Grange membership was larger than in any other state. The Grange advocated temperance as well as rural free mail delivery and gave funds to the University of Maine. It has always been nonpartisan and has been an important influence for women banding together for voting

Ocean View Grange, Tenants Harbor. *Nasser K.*

rights. Long before the ratification of the Nineteenth Amendment to the Constitution in 1920, the Grange granted women equal voting rights within the organization. Four of the elected positions in each local Grange could only be held by women, and any teenager old enough to draw a plow was encouraged to participate. During World War II, the Grange bought war bonds and supported men and women in the armed forces by sending packages of food and clothing.

The Ocean View Grange No. 463 was founded in 1906 by twenty-four men and thirty-four women. They met in rental halls until they could afford to build a Grange Hall. The Ocean View Grange has a large room downstairs for community events, like art shows, public bean suppers (free for veterans), an annual flea market and so forth. Up the picturesque typical Maine stairs with high risers and narrow treads is the meeting room for official meetings. Anywhere in Maine, a Grange has to keep a membership of eight to stay open. Many have closed, but the Ocean View Grange Hall was rescued by the community and restored (new roof, floor, plastering). It has a busy calendar of annual good works, including road clean-up, placing American flags on military veterans' graves each Memorial Day, providing food and supplies to the animal shelter, helping pay for heating oil for families in need in St. George and providing dictionaries to third graders at the St. George School in a Words for Thirds program. The Grange is not specific to any religion, although the reading that opens the meeting usually comes from the Bible. "I joined to save the building when I moved here from Ohio," said Larry N. Bailey, "but the most important aspect is the camaraderie."

Chapter 7

Ice

Robert Frost's short poem "Fire and Ice" conveys the supernatural power, almost black magic, of ice:

Some say the world will end in fire,
Some say in ice.
From what I've tasted of desire
I hold with those who favor fire.
But if it had to perish twice,
I think I know enough of hate
To say that for destruction ice
Is also great
And would suffice.

I used to walk to the remains of an ice business on a lake in Litchfield, Connecticut. Visible here was where ice was cut, the icehouses where it was stored and where the ice slid down onto the barges. It looked like and was serious business. The ice trade was founded by Frederic Tudor, known as Boston's "Ice King," the United States' first monopolist, who didn't go to Harvard like his two older brothers because of his eagerness for business (he said he was a businessman from age thirteen). Tudor began in 1806 by supplying the rich Europeans in Martinique. Later shipments went to the southern United States and Cuba and eventually to tropical climates and as far as India and China, hundreds of thousands of tons at the height of

Ice harvesting. *Penobscot Bay Marine Museum.*

the ice trade in the 1850s. Henry Thoreau described the ice business thus in *Walden* (1854): "He cuts and saws the solid pond, unroofs the house of fishes, and carts off their very elements and air, held fast by chains and stakes like corded wood, through the favoring winter air to wintry cellars to underlie the summer."

Americans became used to having their drinks iced (which never caught on in France), and some had ice cellars. Ice was harvested from Maine, as well as Massachusetts and the Hudson River Valley, to fill the demand. Ice from Maine was sawed into big blocks and loaded on speedy schooners for the southern seaports, and Maine fish, instead of being dried, was preserved in ice in the late 1800s.

Clifford Ladd in his book about growing up in Rockland in the 1920s, *Steamboats Sleighbells and a One-Man Band*, reminisced about watching the ice harvest at Chickawaukie Lake in north Rockland:

> *The ice houses were big barn-like buildings, built on the shore of the lake. There were inclined wooden ice ways that were built so that ice could be skidded up as high as the layer being filled—one on top of the other, until the house was filled to the top. As each layer was complete, it was covered with sawdust to insulate it. Layer upon layer was done in this fashion and the ice would be kept intact during the summer months.*

Men pushed the floating ice along to the foot of the inclines, where they were skidded up using iron chains. The work was understood to be dangerous from harvesting to transport, and immigrant workers spent all winter in frigid bunkhouses, some unaccustomed to the cold of New York State or New England.

The ice man as Ladd describes him wore a rubber apron on his shoulders to protect him from the ice as he carried it, and at the base of his apron there were two pockets to trap the water before it dripped onto the kitchen floor.

Ice was cut from Chickawaukie Lake from January to March. It was stored in large barns, insulated between each block with sawdust. In 1877, a large icehouse was built at the south end of the lake. The ice was stored until spring and summer, when it was delivered to lobstermen, fishermen and farmers. The Rockland Ice Company had icehouses on Chickawaukie and at their wharf on Crockett's Point at the turn of the century to provide ice for their fish-packing and wholesale fruit and produce businesses. According to Ann Morris's *History of Blackington's Corner and the Highlands*, unlike the ice from other parts of Maine, which was shipped to the South and abroad, the Chickawaukie ice was used locally. That did not mean the ice was meager, though. In the *Courier-Gazette* of February 9, 1892, an article titled "The Midst of the Ice Harvest" had this note:

> *The local ice men are now in the very midst of the exhilarating task of filling their houses, and available men and teams are hard at work.... Marsh & Case, at Chickawaukie Pond, had thirty men and eight horses at work Saturday filling the 3,000-ton house at the pond. The ice is 14 inches thick, free from snow, and first class in every particular.*

The commercial ice companies allowed dairy farmers who backed up to the lake from Old County Road to cut ice for themselves at night, "by moon light and touch-light, and later by strings of electric lights which made the lake look like a winter carnival."

My neighbor on St. George, distinguished artist of local scenes and town coffin maker Marvon Hupper, recalls his father taking him as a young boy out to a pond where ice was being harvested: "Ice was being hauled to Port Clyde by horse which I watched. Before my time, it was also slid down to Port Clyde on a sluice that my uncle Myron Hupper said he used to skate on as a boy. Some believe there was a sluice to slide it down to the point."

The ice was spring fed and clear. I have a paper where my great-grandfather Mark Marshall gave an ice company the right to haul the ice across his farm to the point. When I was young, my grandparents had an eight-by-ten-inch yellow card to put in the window of the farm to let the ice man know they needed ice. When I was very young, I went with Dad to buy ice in Port Clyde. It was in an old barn with part of the roof missing on, I believe, the road to Marshall Point.

The Mid-Coast had ice to spare. Cyrus Eaton in his history noted that the ice was so thick in the Penobscot Bay in 1875 that sleighs crossed from Vinalhaven to Islesboro and Lincolnville, and the Bangor steamship *Katahdin* was frozen in the ice at Belfast until April.

Chapter 8

Marshall Point

Counting Owls Head, in and around the St. George Peninsula are four lighthouses, an indication of tricky or treacherous surrounding waters and beautiful to behold. The Tenants Harbor Light is situated on one of the most picturesque scenes in Maine and is the home of its owner, Jamie Wyeth. Owls Head is a majestic sight from the water and a delightful climb up a path and inside it to panoramic views. The oldest lighthouse of St. George is on Whitehead Island in the Penobscot Bay.

Marshall Point is like the lighthouse in a snow globe. There are two ways to reach it by land. Beginning on Route 131 East, look for a square granite house at the left just before Drift Inn Beach Road two miles after Tenants Harbor and one mile before Port Clyde and the tip of the peninsula. Proceed through the stone pillars, the surf flying up at your left, to the parking lot of Marshall Point. Or go up the hill on Factory Road that borders the center of Port Clyde and turn right. That has the finest view of the harbor. Arriving either way, the Penobscot Bay meets the St. George River, and the Marshall Point Light stands vigil.

In 1789, the United States Lighthouse Service was established by George Washington. Four years later, the Town of St. George was established. The land for the lighthouse was purchased by the government from Samuel Marshall Jr. in 1831. The steady hand of Samuel Sr. had guided the family to settle in St. George, and through his father's values, Samuel Jr. knew it was the proper thing to place the lighthouse for the benefit of future mariners.

In 1832, the Marshall Point rubblestone light and keeper's house was built; the light was provided by seven fixed lard oil lamps, each with a fourteen-

Marshall Point. *Aidan Kaczynski.*

inch reflector, all pointing out to sea. The present lighthouse dates from 1858 and is of brick over a foundation of granite, with the lantern built out on a ramp at the water's edge. Lightning destroyed the keeper's house in 1895, and a new house was built. Until about 1937, the ramp was like a little covered bridge to protect the fuel the keeper carried to the light.

The next improvements included the addition of the fog bell tower with bronze bell; a weather mast, which was innovative for its time; and a telephone. One individual, Charles Skinner, a Civil War veteran, held the position of keeper of Marshall Point Light for forty-five years, from 1874 to 1919. Electricity modernized the lighthouse in 1935, but there was still a kerosene oil wick lamp for standby (the oil storage house of granite remains on the grounds). The lighthouse ceased to have a light keeper after it was fully automated in 1971. The Fresnel lens was removed by the Coast Guard and replaced by an LED light in 2018. If there is a power failure, a battery back-up keeps the lighthouse lit. The original lens disappeared mysteriously years ago, but most of the lenses are at the museum, including the "Barrel Lens," which is on display in the Octagon Room.

Marshall Point came to fame as Forrest Gump's farthest destination from home in the eponymous movie (1994), the point where he turned around to run back. Forrest reminisces on his front porch in Alabama what had made him get up from his rocking chair, run for no particular reason and keep going to the Santa Monica Pier in San Francisco and then Port Clyde, Maine, and most of the way back again. Forrest makes an immortal speech about the existential attitude toward living: "When I got to another ocean, I figured since I'd gone that far, well, I might as well turn back and keep on going. When I got tired, I slept. When I got hungry, I ate. When I had to go, you know, I went."

Forrest stopped running for no particular reason, just as he had begun. Naturally, he stopped to sleep during the two years it took. And then, plucking the romantic chord in most of us, he admits shyly that he thought a lot during his personal marathon. "Most of all I thought about Jenny."

People were inspired to run a distance alongside Forrest in the movie, and in real life, marathon runners have attempted to repeat the feat. The first person to complete the run Forrest Gump did was a British veterinarian, Rob Pope. He started in Mobile in September 2016 and followed the route of Forrest across the southern states to Santa Monica and then east, across eighteen states, reaching the Marshall Point Light on April 28, 2017 (he completed a third crossing in September). Dr. Pope did know why he was running, which was for charity, to benefit the World Wildlife Fund and Peace Direct.

The Marshall Point Museum is not to be missed. The volunteers who curate the collection are ready to lend depth to what is displayed. Visitors emerge dazzled and spouting lore. The Nautical Ships Quilt, mounted on one wall, is by the Port Clyde Baptist Church Sewing Circle. On another wall are mounted doll-sized buoys corresponding to those of the present lobster fishermen of St. George. (Martinsville, where I live, although not the closest to the Port Clyde commercial harbor, has the most fishermen of any village.) The buoys are quite exact in reproducing the coloring of the schooners. They are the artistry of Dana Smith, one of the founders of the museum. When artist Kathleen Fox paints a picture for a fisherman of his boat, if she doesn't get the colors just so, the fisherman will bring his buoy as a sample.

My favorite items in the Marshall Point Museum relate to women's work. One is a pair of antique fisherman's mittens knit from what looks like twine and worn by three generations. Such mittens, hand-tailored to suit fishermen of Maine, Nova Scotia and Labrador for over one hundred years, are designed to be worn wet. They are boiled before use and soaked repeatedly in salt water to shrink the wool fibers until they mold to the fisherman's hands. When a man went out lobstering, he took his mittens

Above: Quilt at Marshall Point Museum. *Aidan Kaczynski.*

Left: Mittens that lasted. *Aidan Kaczynski.*

off a nail on the boat (they had loops on their cuffs), dipped them in warm water from the engine, wrung them out well and put them on wet. Then he began hauling traps or working with bait. There is also a large spinning wheel, at least a yard in diameter. Thankful Arey Teel and Rufus Teel

Miniature buoys of St. George fishermen. *Marshall Point Museum/Aidan Kaczynski.*

Snapshot of Tom Hanks in the production of the movie *Forrest Gump*. *Marshall Point Museum/ Aidan Kaczynski.*

once lived on Teel Island. They had fourteen children, so how Thankful had time to spin is a wonder. Thankful lived until age seventy-two (1915), and Rufus died at ninety-five in 1934, whereupon N.C. Wyeth painted a fantasy world of Teel called *Island Funeral*, available in reproduction as a five-hundred-piece puzzle.

This is a very accessible lighthouse, and in fair weather, people are gamboling about like in a Maurice Prendergast painting. The keeper's barn has recently been restored, and the volunteer organization is dedicated to keeping Marshall Point shipshape.

Chapter 9

Sarah Orne Jewett

Sarah Orne Jewett, one of the great nineteenth-century American writers, summered in the village of Martinsville. Her hometown was South Berwick, just up from Portsmouth, New Hampshire, where she assisted her father, a country doctor, on his rounds and rarely saw days with the peace to write. Jewett was a sophisticated, independent woman who went to Boston and Europe and had friends among the literati of her day. But her social milieu branched out to include all types of people, and she fictionalized Martinsville on the St. George Peninsula in a series of her stories.

She introduces characters in vignettes of country life who are connected as if by strawberry runners. They are resilient and empathetic. She observed and recorded country life in a fishing village with detail and verisimilitude. The voices are a phonetic transcription of Maine coast speech. If you listened to her stories read aloud all night, you would expect to awake to the post–Civil War period in Maine when she wrote them.

It is uncertain if she literally wrote in the one-room schoolhouse that is still just before the bend of the road in Martinsville, but she did go there to sit and muse, while staying in the Anchorage, a cottage nearby, and close to the room from which she watched the boats sail past. Jewett loved to travel. She had already been to Martinsville as a guest of her Boston publisher friends the Thomas Aldriches when she and her friend Annie Fields returned there on holiday. This was after sailing on the Aldriches' yacht to the Caribbean.

One-room schoolhouse, now a private home, associated with S.O. Jewett. *Nasser K.*

(It is wrong to imagine Jewett as dainty. When the yacht made landfall in Nassau, the other female passengers were carried to shore, while Jewett jumped right into the water and made her way unaided.) By 1890, the Aldriches had bought a house on Harts Neck, and other summer people followed. Meanwhile, Jewett and Mrs. Fields knew that Tenants Harbor offered the serene retreat of a coastal village.

Jewett had an unparalleled knack for depicting quiet lives. She called her imaginary village "Deephaven" in the sketches she had published in the *Atlantic Monthly* by 1880. *The Country of Pointed Firs*, her most famous novel, came later, serialized, and was set in a fictive place on the Maine coast, identified only as "Dunnet Landing"—"somewhere along the shore between Tenants Harbor and Boothbay." When an illustrated edition of the novel came out in 1919, photographs for it were taken on the St. George Peninsula.

The stories and *The Country of Pointed Firs* are quiet, humorous and tender but stark. Jewett confects a whole vignette from how a fairly old woman rows out to an island where her mother lives, and the mother signals long

Bay view from where Jewett vacationed in Martinsville. *Nasser K.*

before the daughter arrives. In another story, *Poor Joanna*, a bride jilted on her wedding day leaves all her belongings to her brother and takes off with meager possessions for a deserted island, where she lives quite well as a total hermit the rest of her days. Jewett could have modeled her after the contemporary bachelor hermit of Hermit's Island, Albert Morse, who planted crops and sold the wool of his sheep, except Joanna banishes sheep and brought chickens.

In a subtle story titled "Marsh Rosemary," a solitary woman, Ann Floyd, enters the scene sewing by her favorite window: "She sat in a straight-backed, splint-bottomed kitchen chair, and always put back her spool with a click on the very same spot on the window-sill." She is hoping a certain young man will stop by, and indeed, Jerry Lane appears leaning over her fence. Potentiality animates her, and she experiences delight and love, until the young man goes off to sea and two-times her. Ann believes Jerry has drowned in a shipwreck, but then she hears he has been seen up the coast and goes to hunt him down and reclaim him. But she looks in the window at the man she waited for faithfully and sees him now a family man with wife and child. The other woman looks happy with Jerry, and having a child might have brought out the best in him. Ann Floyd shrugs, turns around and goes home reconciled to the life she had before he entered.

I know something of the material culture that went into Jewett's stories and the love stories. For instance, I am reminded of my strong, self-sufficient grandmother, her Bible reading and study of Latin and the care she gave to her garden. My grandmother sat down many evenings at the piano to play hymns and American folk tunes. Watching this admired person, I saw her sometimes sadden. Family had warned not to interrupt her reveries, though. If she shed a tear, I was told, she was thinking of her first husband, a soldier who died of influenza just after World War I.

There is a T-shirt that has appeared sometimes in the general stores of St. George that reads, "Port Clyde [or Tenants Harbor], the town where nothing happens." Continuity and peace after the United States had been torn by the Civil War required women's seeking back to old ways—their herbs, their gardens, their crafts. Jewett wrote, for instance, of another Mid-Coast mythical village:

> *Deephaven is utterly out of fashion. It never recovered from the effects of the embargo of 1807, and a sand-bar has been steadily filling in the mouth of the harbor. Though the fishing gives what occupation there is for the inhabitants of the place it is by no means sufficient to draw recruits from abroad. But nobody in Deephaven cares for excitement, and if some one once in a while has the low taste to prefer a more active life, he is obliged to go elsewhere in search of it, and is spoken of afterward with kind pity.*

This part of the world miniaturized the good in the larger world for Jewett; both the quaintness and natural beauty charmed her. "We often heard quaint words and expressions which we never had known anywhere else but in old books. There was a great deal of sea-lingo in use. Everything in Deephaven was more or less influenced by the sea (including the minister's sermons)."

She capped her magical summer with an elegiac tone. "The sunshine of a northern summer was coming to its lovely end," and she let each day

> *slip away unwillingly as a miser spends his coins. I wished to have one of my first weeks back again, with those long hours when nothing happened except the growth of herbs and the course of the sun. Once I had not even known where to go for a walk; now there were many delightful things to be done and done again, as if I were in London. I felt hurried and full of pleasant engagements, and the days flew by like. Handful of flowers flung to the sea wind.*

Wharf at the harbor of Port Clyde. *Nasser K.*

to get snaggle-toothed about how casually the cars were chained onto ferries as our family drove up and down the East Coast. He would applaud the state ferries of Maine.

The two boats of the Monhegan Ferry Service go back and forth from Port Clyde. The choice of times from mid-May to the end of September allows tourists to go on day trips either to Monhegan or far out in the bay to watch the puffin gambol in the waves. In fall to spring, service shifts to once a day. Poets, naturalists, artists and even John Smith, the Pilgrim who raised a crop of lettuce on the island, have sung Monhegan's praises, and tourists who go there leave their automobiles behind in the parking area near the Port Clyde General Store. The trip one way takes seventy minutes in the *Laura B* and fifty in the *Elizabeth Ann*.

The older boat, the *Laura B*, is sixty-five feet long and rigged as a heavy-duty workboat. Built in 1943 in Solomons, Maryland, its first use was military. It was designated U.S. Army T-57, one of 150 T boats that transported troops and supplies. T-57 spent World War II in the Pacific in the sea of the Philippines. The *Laura B* carried two .50-caliber machine guns on deck and came under fire while doing patrol duty. The vessel was brought to Maine by Clyde Bickford in 1946 to transport lobsters from Vinalhaven to Boston and New York City. He gave it his wife's name, which it kept after it was changed

Top: Harbor of Port Clyde. *Bottom*: Port Clyde view. *Nasser K.*

to a mail boat in 1952. Jim and his son Andy Barstow began the Monhegan Boat Line in 1978 with the *Laura B.*

When the boat's roof was replaced, there were found seven-millimeter bullets in it. This historic boat is a thoroughly fit vessel. It is one of the last of the T boats that still runs, thanks to refurbishing and assiduous and outstanding maintenance.

The smoother ride is on Port Clyde's other mail boat to Monhegan, the *Elizabeth Ann*. The *Elizabeth Ann*, launched in 1995, is the same size as its predecessor but offers more tourist-friendly features of a choice of seating—in the heated glassed-in cabin, on the covered stern or on the sightseeing deck.

The ferry from Port Clyde goes on a more limited schedule to Matinicus, the most seaward island of the bay, twenty-two miles offshore. The reason is not only few passengers but also the fact that the ferry has to come and go on high tide and between daylight. Penobscot Island Air has flights as well.

Edna St. Vincent Millay was inspired by Matinicus, and even living in Brooklyn, she was drawn to water views. Millay wrote:

> *We were very tired, we were very merry—*
> *We had gone back and forth all night on the ferry.*

Chapter 11

Fishing Heritage

When St. George was a hinterland, before anybody was sure if it belonged to England or France, fish was dried on its shores. Fish were a staple that also was sought by settlers like the Pilgrims down in Plymouth. Rockland pushed forward with the lime industry, while St. George remained very rural. Then late in the nineteenth century, the granite quarries employed hundreds of men, many immigrants from Ireland, Scandinavia, Scotland and Italy. By the 1930s, the New England quarries had closed, and fishing was the dominant industry on the peninsula. Fish had been very plentiful. This is what had brought Europeans since the time of John Cabot, when the seamen only had to lower their weighted baskets into the water to hoist them up loaded with a catch. Then ground fishing declined and fish processing became important.

Fishing is bred into a person from constantly being around it. Bert Witham is a multigenerational lobsterman and close friend of both the late Andrew and Jamie Wyeth. Bert's great-grandfather, grandfather and father were fishermen, and he and his son are. Bert's grandfather ran away from home at eighteen and captained a schooner out of Key West. He knew Teddy Roosevelt, who stood him $10,000 to start a lobster business in Rockland. The father built one pound in Tenants Harbor, maintained it and moved on to establish fishing ventures along the coast. Bert was ten or eleven when his father bought an outboard for him. Bert and his grandfather built ten traps, and Bert set them out in Rockland Harbor, where he would fish after school and on weekends. He remembered:

Mostly my mother went with me until by twelve to fourteen a friend went along with me. The family owns Green Island, and I'm the fourth generation to fish around it. My grandfather got up at five, and one time my father got up late and my grandfather left him behind. My father got into a dory and rowed seventeen miles from Rockland to Green Island. His mother watched him as he passed Owls Head Lighthouse. She couldn't stop him.

My grandfather would say, "Go get us a haddock for dinner," and my father would row out and catch one close to the island. Other times he would lie in the skiff with a bottomless bucket and spear flounders for dinner. My father also gave me a treble hook, which worked surprisingly well with jigging codfish, that were attracted by the brightness.

My father started out packing trash fish that women preserved in jars. My ex-wife and I were living in a cottage down at Tenants Harbor when one morning my father came with a load of logs. He said, "You're going to build a dock." There were thirty logs twenty feet long. Next day, my father came with iron rods and a hand drill, so I started building the wharf. The first year completed one section out of six, twenty by twenty feet, and a storm took it away. Then I built another section; this time I weighed it down with the rock, and that held it. It took thirteen years to build the wharf to two hundred feet. Prock Marine from Rockland helped me complete it at the end. I bought lobsters, and when I married Donni, she ran the wharf while I was at sea.

Bert sold his house and wharf to Linda Bean, who also owns the Port Clyde General Store and the Dip Net Restaurant, which overlook the wharf. When Bert was young, there was no trap limit. The minimum size of lobsters that can be fished keeps increasing to save the population. It used to be okay if you wanted to catch other fish just to do it. The same boat could drag for scallops, sein for herring or get rigged up to catch shrimp. Now there is a commercial license for each catch.

Groundfishing is still pursued between Portland and the Canadian border, a tide coastline of 3,478 miles. In 2007, the Midcoast Fishermen's Cooperative created Port Clyde Fresh Catch, the first of what is now many dozen community-supported fisheries in the United States. According to an October 2012 article by Patricia Leigh Brown in the *New York Times*:

Port Clyde Fresh Catch was born in crisis. Fishing is woven into the warp and weft of daily life here, a place where the water seems more dominant than the land. The village's working waterfront still resembles a Wyeth,

Rockland, Maine street. *Rockland Historical Society*.

> *alive with aging trawlers, lobster traps and weatherworn shacks dwarfed by evergreens. But looks can be deceiving: Until recently, the picturesque occupation beloved by "people from away," as summer residents are called, was on the verge of collapse.*

Fresh Catch eliminated the middleman and offered a steadier income to fishermen who also banded together for responsible marine conservation, like redesigning their nets to allow juvenile fish to escape. Said Julia Merrill, a part-time lobsterman, "Some of the fishermen are boisterous and some mellow, and the energy of the crews differs, but they all love what they do. They don't want their independent lifestyle to go away."

Chapter 12

Knitting for Fisherfolk

From religious paintings, it is known that some sweaters were knit in medieval times in southern Germany and Italy, when much of early knitting was small items of ladies' fancy work such as decorative collars or bags. "Only fishermen took to sweaters," writes Richard Rutt in *A History of Hand-Knitting*. To that we can add woolen mittens as well.

The purpose of the fisherman's sweater was to provide a tough working garment that protected him from the bitter elements at sea. Fishermen's sweaters came in various forms and fashions, from patterned guernsey (or gansey) sweaters knit with a tightly twisted yarn to striped Breton sweaters (the stripes helpful to those trying to spot sailors out at sea) to solid knit naval or polar expedition sweaters issued as uniforms. Knitted goods and patterns were exchanged via trade routes established in the seventeenth century. Seafarers developed their own sweater designs and simple shapes that were insulating and practical. Many fishermen, of course, knit, as did the women waiting for their return.

Knitting had the advantage of being work that a person could pick up and lay down between other duties, thus the expression still colloquial in Maine, "to knit the time." According to John Gould's *Maine Lingo*, "Sharpening fence stakes can be knitting work between the maple season and plowing. The making of nets, bait bags, and lobster-pot heads is also knitting in this sense of an odd-moment task."

In one searing act of *Riders to the Sea* by Irish playwright J.M. Synge, the sweater of the dead fisherman identifies the fifth and last son of the family.

Ivan Bly of Martinsville. He wears a pair of sweaters knitted by his partner, Heather, the way he wears them when fishing, one over the other. *Nasser K.*

This idea sprang from a funeral that Synge observed in the Aran Islands of a young man lost at sea. It was once thought that initials were knit into designs to identify a sailor, but this was likely a myth perpetuated in literature. Rather, the patterns of fishing sweaters are thought to have delighted and challenged knitters and identified their communities. The designs on Scottish sweaters were arranged vertically, while Hebridean patterns consist of a horizontal design across the chest and a vertical one below. Patterning of cables or knit-and-purl structures are not only a design element but also provide a greater level of warmth, pocketing air beneath the surface. The supply list for Ernest Shackleton's 1907–09 Antarctica expedition included inner and outer clothing of 100 percent wool garments. The explorer himself was photographed wearing a hand-knit turtleneck sweater in plain stitch except for on the upper chest and collar, which were knit in a basket-weave pattern.

According to Gail DeMeyere, museum curator and sweater designer, the changes in construction and design of the fisherman sweater have been subtle. Some related to whether the sweaters were tucked into trousers. Sleeves could be knit from the top down, which made it easier to rip back the worn parts and reknit the sleeves in whatever color or thickness was available. Maine artisan Marilyn Robinson sees a lot of fisherman's knit sweaters in her upcycling business, Jack and Mary Designs, specializing in fashion-forward accessories made from recycled sweaters. The biggest change she sees is that older sweaters were made from wool that still had lanolin or oil in the fibers. "The sweaters seemed almost waterproof," she observed. "And the knit was much denser. The older sweaters if they were cardigans always had leather buttons with metal shanks, and their cable patterns were usually based on local Irish designs. The newer sweaters I see are still made from wool but have a looser knit and a variety of cable patterns."

Some men wear a good sweater as Sunday best, not a suit, in St. George. I have watched a girl of eighteen working in a yarn shop in Rockland and knitting a sweater as a commission for a fisherman. She explained to me that he wanted it just so—a certain length of the cuffs, rather tight at the sleeves that would extend only to the wrists. He had in mind an image of an ideal fisherman's sweater, which was also what his father and grandfather before him had worn. It looked gigantic, and she said she would have to felt it in scalding water when it was completed to shrink it half down to his size. She had already repaired the sweater of another member of the crew, and her present client was the sternman who saw her work. The idea of a garment

Ivan Bly. *Nasser K.*

that is worn for work over many years and is beautiful is as essential to a fisherman sweater as its design.

The St. George Peninsula has knitting and quilting parties for women, with some of the women executing designs they learned as girls and some knitting designs. Some lucky lobstermen are knitted sweaters, caps, socks and vests. The felted wool dolls dressed to fish, sold by the annual Baptist Church Sewing Circle, wear Aran or rolled-neck style. The Sewing Circle created the "Lobsterette," a female lobsterman with a red sweater and red knit hat. Maggie Davis, wife of a Port Clyde fisherman, knits for him and is one of the peninsula's master knitters. She says her wristlets (fingerless mittens) keep a man's hands from being sore under the oilcloth. The wristlets are boiled and shrunk before wearing. Maggie's wristlets are popular with women too.

I heard my neighbor up the road, Ivan Bly, building something and went to his barn. "Ivan," I said, "do you ever wear a sweater out fishing?"

Ivan typifies a Maine fisherman in ways that are true and good: self-reliant, direct, assured, competent at many skills, independent-minded and with warm ties to family and the community.

"My girlfriend made me one," he said. Would he pose in it for my book? "Sure."

"How will my friend who is taking the photographs find you?" (I was thinking of how during the day fishermen are at sea.)

Ivan picked up a long piece of cardboard. He cut a piece from the cardboard and penciled his phone number. Then he grinned. Before giving me the cardboard, he took a fixed-blade knife and carved the cardboard off again. "Here," he said, "I'll make a business card out of it."

Chapter 13

Quarries

The poet Robert Frost's "Mending Wall" calls us to respect our neighbors and accept change (even of stone walls). New England's fieldstone and its walls are its great symbols. It is pleasant to drive by them or, closer up, to be entertained by squirrels and chipmunks that race up and down them and do preposterous acrobatics even in winter when they should quiet down. Stone walls trace lacy patterns around rural properties of New England, where once sheep and farm animals and now more likely deer, porcupines, turkeys, muskrats and so forth abide.

According to Albert J. Smalley (*St. George, Maine: A Ramble through the Town*), stone walls are the most "conclusive and enduring records" of early land divisions, evidence that "adjoining owners agreed that the wall indicated the correct division line. In many cases walls appear to be the result of joint efforts of the owners. It is safe to say that although a wall is not always the answer and may be in the wrong place because of obvious reasons, in the main it was a correct boundary."

However, the stone walls around my little house have a different functioning: they are a museum. A previous owner collected dozens of antique tools used in quarrying, fishing and railroading here on the peninsula and laid them hither and thither on the stone walls.

Maine was made of granite. Mountains rose up and were folded, and igneous matter was crystallized into rock. In the late nineteenth century, the grandeur of granite ennobled architecture and caught the imagination of the well-heeled. A distinct advantage was that stone could be loaded on boats right at hand, although eventually little railroads were laid from certain quarries to the wharves to transport the thousands of tons of stone.

Much of the work of the quarries was done by hand. For many years, hundreds of workers were employed in the quarries and lived on St. George. The managers of the operations were lodged in small houses, some extant north of Tenants Harbor. Essentially, the work meant drilling even holes in the granite, into which small wedges or pins were hammered. In the quarry at Long Cove, up to twenty-five workers were employed. Some drilled, some broke the stone and some workers could do it all. A holder and several strikers formed a "blasthole team." According to Albert J. Smalley's *History of St. George* (1976), a top drill holder was viewed as the elite of the workmen, due to his steady hand and courage. To make the blasthole, first a pointed chisel or hand drill made a depression in the granite ledge. Then the holder sat on a keg filled with water. A little water was allowed to trickle from an opening in the bottom of the keg to the point of the drill to prevent stone dust from clogging the drill. Then the holder put the drill bit in the hole, a sack having been wound loosely around the drill to keep chips from flying. Now the strikers tapped the drill and the holder turned it. The bit cut into the stone, and that and the force of the strikers broke the stone.

Immigrants from Italy, Finland, Sweden, Ireland and Scotland were among those employed, and many brought their families. The Italian stonecutters taught their skill, and so many English stonecutters were attracted to the granite industry here that part of Long Cove was called Englishtown. Before 1874, a working day extended eleven or twelve hours, but that year, the U.S. government passed a ten-hour working day and set the first decent fee for stoneworkers, $4.25 for an eight-hour day.

Pink granite came from the island of Vinalhaven, while the granite found in the numerous quarries along Long Cove, Tenants Harbor and Clark Island ranges from shades of medium to dark gray to black and is described as having medium to fine texture.

Long Cove Quarry, which opened in 1873, in 1905 measured one thousand feet north to south by five hundred feet east to west and had a depth of twenty to seventy-five feet. It was the only quarry in New England that used tunneling and explosives. The transport of the granite was by an inclined track to a wharf, whence at first schooners and later steel barges carried the stone away. Granite from this quarry was used mostly for monuments and cemeteries in New York and Philadelphia.

The St. George Granite Company, 90 West Street, New York, operated the Willards Point or Wildcat Quarry, which was in Tenants Harbor a mile south of Long Cove. The stone quarried was fine textured and medium gray. Transport was thirty feet to the dock. The Rockland Post Office was made of Wildcat granite, while most of the stone from this quarry was used for paving since it was difficult stone to work; the "rift" grain was not at right angles to the "north–south" grain, making it impossible to break the stone in squares and leaving a lot of waste stone, which is left in the woods today.

Spruce Head quarries supplied many buildings of the East, such as the post offices of Pittsburgh, Atlanta and Bar Harbor. Many tons of Spruce Head granite were conveyed on the sloop *Yankee Girl* (from the Casco Bay) to the Rockland Breakwater in 1891.

It is interesting that the stone had to be pried open, rather like opening a clamshell, and then cut and harvested. Smalley described the intuition it took in addition to strength: "An experienced man can in most cases tell by the feel of a piece of granite how the grain runs. The grain (rift) usually runs in an easterly westerly direction perpendicular to the horizon. Another grain, known as the hard way, is at right angles to the rift, or east–west grain. A third grain (lift) is parallel with the horizon."

Blocks of cut granite are a dramatic sight rising in a wall of about seventy-five feet alongside Route 131 East (Port Clyde Road), but after ascending a few jagged blocks, I sensed it was not a normal climbing experience and came back down. Relics of the quarrying can be seen by walking onto Clark Island (with permission, as it is private property), not far from where there is a waterspout that rises if you arrive at just the right hour of high tide. More accessible is a quarry that is now a very deep, pristine pond. For some, it is a swimming hole, but quarries are notoriously perilous for swimmers.

Granite blocks that look as though they have a Greek key pattern burned in from the marks made prying them are in profusion at the edge of Drift Inn Beach. The rusty antique tools strewn on my home's stone walls look like props for a Hieronymus Bosch painting. Of the immigrant populations who worked in the quarries, the Finns built a small library at Long Cove (later sold to a Harold Watts and moved to his farm nearby). The library was an offshoot of the temperance movement, and concerts were also held there. The Finnish Church was built in 1917, and its parsonage is now a Finnish heritage center.

Chapter 14

Ridge Road, Martinsville

Ridge Road is a fingernail moon on the finger of the St. George Peninsula running north to south from Port Clyde Road to Turkey Cove. It has houses of the fisherfolk and the Ridge Baptist Church, established in 1817. Jogging on Ridge from my house, which, like a lot of the houses on it, is on a dirt road off from it, I not only encounter turkeys, osprey, hares and deer but also local people who like to walk. "I'll see you on the street," said Noah Bly, the blacksmith on Ridge who creates wrought-iron objects at his forge and keeps goats as pets for his children.

A pair of ospreys leaves the high trees after raising their brood, but they return and, when obliged, build a new nest. Some days, I glory in the Acadian beauty. Other days I just listen, to chickens and roosters scooting around their coops, frogs, songbirds and the little creatures that displace leaves as they go about their activities. The difference between seeing a turkey and seeing all the things it can do is like when I looked up and saw Shaquille O'Neal towering over me at the end of a supermarket aisle and watching him play ball. These turkeys sometimes will waddle right next to me. They can come crashing down as a group from high in the pines. I've seen them all arranged in a circle and the small ones twirling around in a ragged circle around a huge fanning one, whose great whoosh as he shifts the angle of his feathers is what draws my attention first. I find I can't promise sighting wildlife to my guests, but they have sometimes been on the spot for interesting views. Like the sort of meteor showers of dragonflies, gobbling up mosquitoes one likes to think; and the Arctic hares that by mid-summer will come up to the deck

Above: Ridge Church. *Nasser K.*

Left: Ridge Church by N.C. Wyeth. *Wyeth Foundation for American Art.*

from curiosity or chase a blueberry thrown their way and that in winter are only visible as two watchful eyes in a pelt of white fur.

St. George being a narrow peninsula, it is like an island, not rich in species of mammals, though we see a panoply of migratory birds. Usually only moose footprints are seen on St. George. Then one Labor Day, my son was visiting and took a bike ride, turning from Ridge Road up Turkey Cove and then left at Walston Road, the other east–west road on the peninsula. He and a moose almost ran into each other. Lucky!

Turning off onto a lane that divides the two parts of the Ridge Baptist Church cemetery leads to the prospect that N.C. Wyeth painted. On the peninsula, other beautiful small churches are still in use. The Tenants Harbor Baptist Church, remodeled by Stephens and Cobb of Portland and

W.H. Glover of Rockport, was dedicated in 1891. The Port Clyde Christian Church was designed by the Arctic explorer and astronomer Russell O. Porter, who built at Port Clyde some little innovative houses at the end of land. He played a part in designing the telescope at Mount Palomar and has craters named after him on the moon and Mars.

Both the latter churches are noted for their stained-glass windows. The chancel window at the Baptist church, sixteen feet by nine feet, represents the Samaritan woman at the well, pitcher in hand, listening to Christ who is throned on a big rock. The windows of the Port Clyde Christian Church have many religious figures and motifs, among them a parley of colorfully dressed Native Americans with European explorers and a young St. George. triumphing over a fallen dragon.

Chapter 15

Stone Walls

The Native Americans used stone walls for mounds, foundations and fishing weirs, and perhaps also for defensive bulwarks, but they did not use them to create boundaries between properties; it was the immigrants from the British Isles who brought the tradition of boundary walls, which had been built in Wales and Scotland for at least three thousand years.

The St. George Peninsula provides abundant stones perfect for stone walls. A good stone wall is 20 percent granite; stone walls on St. George are 40 percent granite, the rest a variety of mostly sedimentary rocks. New England has at least twenty kinds of granite. For example, Clark Island has a sparkling speckled granite, and black granite is quarried halfway down the peninsula. Granite burst up through magma and cooled, forming mountains. When the New England coast was drowned, all that was left of the mountain range was the peaks—features like the St. George Peninsula or islands of the Penobscot Bay. Thirty to fifteen thousand years ago, the Laurentide ice sheet retreated. It scoured the land down to the bedrock and lifted up billions of stones, which were scattered across the region and left deposits of all sizes of materials. As the ice became thicker, glaciers pushed, scraped and dragged stone. Rivers were born in the fjord-like inlets, which is why Maine is a kayaker's paradise. Granite thus is the crushed remains of this glacial movement of a mile-high front of ice.

The granite is round because it was tumbled. It was hard enough to stay intact. It also may have a flat face when cracked by the force of the ice. When settlers cleared the forest for agriculture in colonial times, the movement of

Stone wall of St. George. *Nasser K.*

rocks continued. The soil froze deeper, and frost pushed more rocks to the surface; then spring rains eroded soil, exposing more rocks, and more stone rose to the surface—a familiar process to New England gardeners!

For some, building a stone wall was just a job; others used the best practices. The double wall—parallel rows of stone filled in with smaller stone—is the epitome and takes craftsmanship. The use of the stone walls was to mark property boundaries or to keep animals from straying. The period when most were built was after the American Revolution until about 1825, so the walls are ruins of early America. The peninsula has had cattle, but running sheep was major. There were sometimes paddocks in colonial times, stone corrals where livestock that had wandered were kept until the town decided who owned them. The bulk of the stone walls on St. George were to keep animals in and protect gardens. Although a sheep can jump high, if it encounters a large lacy wall with spaces and shadows, it can be scared and might not venture to scale it.

If neglected, stone walls get covered with brush and disappear. Kevin Curtin, a professor at the University of Maine, refurbishes rural stone walls on properties abandoned generations earlier. He gestured at the beautiful stone wall he was reclaiming and said, "Life is too short not to do what you love."

Chapter 16

Roads

Historian Smalley accurately likened St. George's roads during a spring frost upheaval to "deep hogwallows." He elaborated:

> *When the warm spring days melted the snow and the frost started out, there would be about two feet of blue clay soup.…Buried rocks and boulders turned into unseen obstructions to wheels and serious dangers to horses' legs. In really bad places the road commissioner tried to better the situation by hauling in and spreading a thick carpet of spruce boughs over the soup.*

In the winter, villagers used to clear the road with their shovels for the mail, two abreast and about fifty yards apart. Eventually, the shovelers coming from different directions met. Early in the twentieth century, the town paid men twenty cents an hour and boys ten cents an hour for shoveling, and if the drifts were lofty, they could always blaze a new path through somebody's field.

In the pages of *The Skipper's Wife*, Mrs. Balano's diary, she wrote about cars getting flat tires going the three or so miles from the tip of St. George—Port Clyde, where the Balanos dwelt—to Tenants Harbor. The reason Ridge Church was built was because members of the congregation didn't have horses and carriages to get to church down at the east side of the peninsula. There are also general stores in three locations of St. George to serve local people, mostly fisherfolk who want to sit and have breakfast with their fellows. For some years, the congregation of the Ridge Church (1839) and

Tenants Harbor Main Street. *St. George Historical Society.*

the Baptist chapel in Port Clyde split the pastor, who went to Port Clyde once a month and held services in the schoolhouse. Port Clyde got its own full-scale church in 1897. This was an interfaith proposition to which the faithful of various denominations contributed. Captain Balano donated the seats, bell, organ and a star window. But the Ridge Church remained the mother church until the Port Clyde church became a separate parish in 1848.

The gravel-topped roads were built beginning before World War I in Rockland and 1914 in St. George. Mud continues to be a trial to the present day for everybody with any sort of drive. Sometimes it seems diabolical how ice, mud, gravel, rocks and dead leaves conspire during Mud Month. A coating of ice by itself presents a lesser problem. One ordinary spring (no flood) in Rockland, the muddy water built up to the point where someone bet that he could row a boat the length of Main Street, and I suppose he did it.

Chapter 17

Local Marble

In cemeteries of Thomaston and, to a lesser extent, the St. George Peninsula are found black marble tombstones. They have become pitted and chalky over the years. Peggy McCrea, who heads the Thomaston Historical Society, has drawn the attention of those who love antiques to these dramatic objects.

While early Thomaston was well known for its production of limestone, an industry responsible for supporting a major percentage of the population, the production of black marble is less known. Marble is a metamorphosed form of limestone that will take a high polish. Early state geological reports referred to local Thomaston marble as "unusually dark and when at the mill, even darker." The original stone takes a shine and is the material of many of the mantelpieces in Thomaston. Most of the stone came from a vein behind Old County Road. It was cut there and floated down the Mill River, now a mere stream, past the east end of today's Thomaston just below Montpelier Mansion to Mill River Village. Here it was milled and carved and polished. Mill River Village was the center of Thomaston/Rockland in the first quarter of the nineteenth century; then the town shifted up.

Black marble from here went as far south as Washington, D.C., where there was an outlet, and Augusta had a black marble fireplace in the statehouse. Today, the Thomaston Historical Society has one, and the Hall Funeral Parlor on Main Street in Thomaston has four of the beautiful marble mantelpieces.

Fireplace of local marble now in Hall Funeral Home, Thomaston. *Nasser K.*

McCrea describes Thomaston marble as "very dark gray with white veins, never mixed with gold or yellow. There were different patterns in shades of white and gray."

In general, fieldstone tombstones are the oldest, followed by slate. The slate can have streaks of white quartz in the plain gray. Next came marble, usually white brought from a distance or sometimes the local Thomaston variety. By late in the nineteenth century, the granite industry had developed, and granite was preferred because of its hardness.

Cyrus Eaton in his 1865 history of the area had this to say about Thomaston marble: "Sullivan Dwight established Mill River as the first successful marble manufactory. He carried on with such spirit and enterprise that Thomaston Marble soon came into fashion and found a ready sale in

Monument on a Thomaston cemetery of local marble. *Nasser K.*

all the principal seaports of the Union." The somber color of this stone had special appeal to Victorians for its suggestion of mourning.

Two cemeteries having some monuments in the stunning Thomaston black marble are in the Thomaston Village Cemetery on Erin/Cemetery Street, which is on the north side of Route 1 (Erin Street is just west of the Thomaston Academy building, which houses the Thomaston Public Library). The first cemetery lane on the right is for the Elm Grove Cemetery, a private cemetery incorporated in 1836. The cemetery has a number of black marble tombstones. To the north lies the Thomaston Village Cemetery, established in the early 1800s. (General Henry Knox's burial plot is off Avenue 1.) The second cemetery lane is alongside the brick building, off Erin Street, three-quarters of the way down on the left (north) side. Fencing surrounds the family plot, which has many black marble monument examples. Peggy McCrea remarked, "A husband and wife may have stones of black marble, but you will notice differences in the striations and patterns, if they were purchased in different time frames from different lots of product."

Chapter 18

Skipper's Wife

Captain Fred Balano and his wife, Dorothea, resided in Port Clyde in a commodious white house on the hill across from the docks in the first half of the twentieth century. *The Log of the Skipper's Wife*, Dorothea Moulton Balano's memoir, edited by her son James W. Balano, recounts the traveling life of a young sea captain's wife between 1910 and 1913, as steamships were replacing schooners in the long-distance cargo trade. For a woman who grew up in Yellow Medicine County, Minnesota, Dorothea adapted outstandingly to life at sea.

She was born in 1882, which makes her six years older than my maternal grandmother. Under normal circumstances, my maternal grandmother was mild and gentle. But when she found me, at about age four, on her cellar steps, making percussive sounds on a glass washboard with a spoon, pretending to be a mermaid plucking a harp, she became distressed. Where had I found that old thing? "Behind the workbench." My grandmother straightened her tall frame. "Generations of women ruined their hands and broke their backs doing the wash with only washboards to help them."

Dorothea Moulton, the "Skipper's Wife," coped with a lot of laundry at sea. She probably had a washboard, not a wringer. Being well off, she must have had help on land, but for twenty years, she did the wash on her husband's four-masted cargo schooner in the Brazil trade and elsewhere. Dorothea was an intellectual and educated. She could apply the trigonometry she learned at the University of Minnesota to navigation. Her diary begins when she went to the Caribbean for a sailing trip, invited

Skipper Balano on his schooner. *Penobscot Marine Museum.*

to chaperone a friend, Betty, whose beau was Captain Balano from Maine. From the first page of the memoir, the reader gathers this is a modern young woman. She states that she didn't look forward to being the "kill-joy, an envious witness to rounds of tickle and slap," and in the course of the diary is uncommonly frank for the era. Her friend did not tolerate the waves and spent a lot of the voyage in her cabin. Meanwhile, Dorothea wrote on July 7, "The Captain cornered me for sunset coffee and stayed on deck with me talking about his home at Port Clyde, Maine. Was he trying to woo? I've nothing to say about what followed....I do wish Betty would get well. It's I, now, who needs the chaperone."

Dorothea succumbed to the advances of the handsome and lusty young sea captain, who was sexually far more experienced than she.

By the end of the voyage, Fred and Dorothea were in love (Betty's affections were taken up with someone else). Dorothea's first sight of the captain's home came after taking the mailboat from Boothbay to Monhegan and Port Clyde, a beautiful spot of granite, rocks, evergreens and much salt water. "Met Captain Archibald, who owns a fleet of coastal steamers. He told me, while Fred was somewhere exploring the boat, that Fred always brought home nice new girls. I replied that during the trip north I had counted over forty-one of them." Dorothea traveled on Fred's boat with him for twenty years, and when the diary ends, she is trying to persuade him to make a voyage to Germany to attend operas.

Still, on board the schooner there was the laundry—so tiresome when she was pregnant with James, something to laugh about (July 27, 1911): "My clothes look lovely, and as they hang on the line over the cabin in the sun to dry seem to attract more attention from the crew than they might receive from landsmen"; and three days later: "Washed clothes again, again, and again, and all through by 10:30."

While at sea, the diary records "temporarily out-lusting" James. She loved her husband very much but didn't hesitate to put forth her own ideas, like her opinion that Fred and his father ought to have accepted the offer to purchase acres of beach property when they docked in Brazil. Dorothea described the moods of the sea and her own moods. Her son James, who edited the diary, is also felt as a warm presence in the book, not shying away from the foibles of the parents he loved.

Chapter 19

Hattie Dunn

At the beginning of World War I, sailing ships were still plying the trade up and down the Eastern Seaboard. The three-masted, 414-ton schooner *Hattie Dunn* had been a coaster for over thirty years when, in May 1918, it was sunk by a U-boat of the Imperial German Navy thirty miles off the New Jersey coast. The mission of U-*151*, commanded by Heinrich von Nostitz und Jänckendorff, was to mine the harbors of Baltimore, Philadelphia and New York, and it was heading up the coast for New York Harbor.

The *Hattie Dunn* did not have a radio; however, the captain and part owner, Charles E. Holbrook of Tenants Harbor, received reassurance before leaving New York Harbor that the area of the coast was clear of German submarines. His ship was "in ballast," or without cargo.

Suddenly, he heard a shot that hit the boat. It seemed to him that an American submarine must be doing target practice. But a second shot followed that was fired right under his bow. As he tried to sail away, shrapnel tore through the riggings. A German-accented English voice called out asking what he was doing. Was he trying to get killed? Captain Holbrook surrendered. The Germans came on board and gave the *Hattie Dunn*'s crew ten minutes to gather their belongings. Meanwhile, bombs were planted in and around the schooner.

The Germans took the crew of seven prisoners and destroyed the ship. Ironically, one of the crew members, the cook, had left Europe after twice being aboard ships that were torpedoed. Von Nostitz brought the *Hattie*

The *Hattie Dunn*. *Marshall Point/Aidan Kaczynski.*

Dunn's crew on board. The captain was polite and patrician in his conduct, which the Americans found more exasperating than gratifying. But by a true coincidence, one of the crewmen of the *Edna*, which the Germans had also destroyed in the same region that May, was a boyhood friend of Holbrook's. It had been thirty years since they had seen each other, and since the Germans were trying to be pleasant to their prisoners, the two men had occasion to catch up. Purportedly, everybody confined on U-*151* found their captors quite genial.

When the German submarine destroyed the steamship *Edna*, that made a total of twenty-three prisoners. This was more than half as many prisoners as the submarine crew. By June, more ships had a deadly meeting with the submarine, which became crowded, so the prisoners were transferred to the lifeboats of two American ships when they were destroyed.

By July 20, after only thirteen weeks and three days at sea, by direct attack or mines, U-boat *151* had destroyed twenty-seven ships. It also captured from an English ship six thousand tons of copper. But the era of the U-boats was over. Many, like U-*151*, had been converted from merchant vessels and were clumsy to operate. For example, it was very slow in its maneuver to sink.

The following is from Captain Holbrook's telling of his story quoted in the November 11, 1939 issue of Rockland's *Courier-Gazette*:

While it was not pleasing to know that my crew and I were prisoners of war, yet, aside from the loss of my ship, there were many moments that I do not recall with bitterness. The treatment received was more than could be expected.... We were accorded many privileges. We were well fed and were not obliged to be penned up in military confinement....During these eight days we had many thrilling experiences. One experience I will never forget, was when we lay at the bottom of the sea off Chincoteague Inlet while the engines of the submarine were being repaired. We were submerged all day. We could hear the propellers of the ships passing overhead. These ships no doubt searched for the German submarine we were in.

Chapter 20

St. George and the Dragon

For over one thousand years, St. George has been venerated for saving a village from the scourge of a dragon that exacted terrible tributes. First, the hungry dragon demanded sheep and was fed one every day until the villagers had no flocks left. Then the dragon feasted on children. One day, St. George, a brave soldier, was riding through the town and saw a young girl being led to the dragon as a sacrifice. St. George vanquished the dragon and rode off with the girl, who naturally adored him.

St. George became the patron saint of England during the reign of Edward III. His courage and courtesy made him a chivalric model to the English. Four English Georges since 1614 have reigned in Britain, and many boys have had the name as well. When two of the great literary figures of England and France, George Eliot and George Sand, wanted a name that wouldn't limit them as writers, they changed their names to George.

When he reached North America, Captain George Weymouth first camped on Monhegan Island and named it George Island. Since Maine must hold a record for the name changes of islands—every new occupant found a reason to immortalize himself—this was not surprising. But the older name of Monhegan—from *Monchiggon* in Algonquin, "out to sea"—stuck, and what Weymouth dubbed the island became the name of the tidal river he explored next: St. George River, flowing down to the sea from St. George Lake in Liberty, Maine. In Thomaston, there is a plaque with a replica of the cross that Weymouth erected when he landed on that section of the river on June 12, 1605.

St. George and the Dragon on St. George Town Office hill. *Nasser K.*

View of St. George. *Nasser K.*

Now to the *St. George and the Dragon* sculpture that sits on the hill under the St. George Town Hall. Children who visit the peninsula with their parents want to get out and scamper around the sculpture. Maybe they want to have their pictures taken with it too because whether they have heard the story or not, they sense the sculpture incarnates courage in protecting the weak.

Dan Daniels made *St. George and the Dragon* in 1980 and, some years later, donated it to the town. Daniels was a welder by trade, and after moving to St. George, his wife's home, he had a radiator repair business. There are two stories of how he got into art. One was that he made a bouquet of radiator caps in his shop and was walking over to his house to give it to his wife when someone stopped his car and asked Dan if he sold sculptures like that. The other is that one time he was asked if he could make a bird sculpture, which he did. Whichever story is the true one, Dan went on from there to a new career for many years.

All the materials he used were recycled metal of different types: tin, stainless steel, old 275-gallon oil barrels as well as old hot water heaters. All the metal was given to him by people or he gathered it up when he saw it around, from about 1978 until 1996.

Randy Elwell was a curious and clever young boy whose family lived next door to the Daniels family. He recalls the period from the late 1970s when Daniels was prolific:

> *Danny was married to my cousin and lived next door as I was growing up. I used to mow their lawn. Towards the end of Danny doing the sculptures, I was helping him by doing the pounding of the pieces of metal, as an old injury from his youth wouldn't let him do a lot of the heavy hammering of the pieces of metal. He gave me his shop, which I took down, and I bought some of his equipment. I think Danny just got ideas and then tackled it. He was also an awesome whittler and carver. I made sculptures until around two or three years ago, until the work wasn't paying for itself. Once in a while I'll make an idea still.*

Chapter 21

Sardine Factory

On the afternoon of September 24, 1970, a devastating fire leveled the Port Clyde Sardine Factory. It was reduced to ashes and rubble, leaving only the name of the street, Factory Road, a graceful descent to the Monhegan Ferry and General Store today and some very artistic sardine tops around the village and in the historical society. Doug Anderson, owner of Doug's Restaurant in Thomaston, whose father managed the plant, said, "There was no trying to put the fire out. It was overwhelming." A minute later, the plant exploded. The explosion blew cans to Hupper's Island without touching down on water.

The fire was so terrible because of the big boilers. There were canning retorts that sterilized at high temperatures cans that went in on racks, for oil or mustard, and cooked the fish. Doug used to go and sit until midnight with the night watchman, Bill Daniels, who watched the boiler gauge all night. When the fire occurred, Doug was in Southwest Harbor heading toward Mount Desert Rock to seine herring. We could look to the west and see the smoke from Port Clyde about seventy miles away.

The sardine factory had been a way of life. Buses went as far as Friendship and Union to pick up women for work. Doug recalled being up with his siblings at five o'clock with their mother. She would wrap gauze and white adhesive tape on her fingers to avoid cutting them on the sharp edges of the tins or with the sharp scissors used to prepare the small oily fish.

Usually there were 125 to 130 women packing. Doug recalled:

Women doing sardine work in the Port Clyde Canning Factory. *Marshall Point/Aidan Kaczynski.*

> *It was like a sorority. There was a comradeship among the women as the women snipped the heads and tails off the tiny fish; they were neighbors who worked together for years. Some women were content with earning minimum wage, but most wanted the piecework rate, which was higher. If they didn't make their quota on piecework, they just got minimum wage. The whistle blew at 7:00 a.m., and the women gathered in the long wooden building by the wharf. They put on their rubber aprons and took their positions in front of the tables and conveyors, two women to a station. Lunch was about thirty-eight minutes, and the workday went to five. The women worked seven to five in season and went on unemployment in the winter. If they brought home fifty dollars a week, they were happy. This was all there was. Once a week, the family went to Rockland. They went Friday night because Friday was payday and bought clothes for the children, provisions and food for the week. The general store was handy but too expensive for staples, if not like Canada, where workers were buying on credit. And the Ernie Ford song applied: "I owe my soul to the company store."*

> *We stayed with our grandmother who lived a block from the general store. Our grandfather was gone most nights catching herring in the coves where the fish went at night. The fishermen went to the coves and netted them and loaded the fish into the carrier. Then the carrier would go to the factory and be pumped out into the tank with refrigerator brine. My father would work long hours helping with pumping out the boats and running the factory by day.*

One thousand families' incomes were affected by the explosion. Many families moved away, some keeping their houses to come back to in the summer because they loved their community. In the early twentieth century, before canning sardines, the Port Clyde Factory pickled herring. These were large sea herring, twelve to fourteen inches, that were scaled and butterflied, backbone removed and put in barrels with vinegar and salt and cured. Port Clyde Sardines as a label moved later to Canada and Poland. Meanwhile, the loss of the factory was very hard for the families where the women had brought in important income to their families.

Barbara Thompson Hupper was employed at the Port Clyde Packing Company, and her metal lunch pail is lent to the St. George Museum by her family. Its contents are as follows: packing card, pay card, scissors for cutting fish, hairnet, tape and a bottle of pain reliever.

Chapter 22

Owls Head Transportation Museum

With 14 working antique planes as well as 150 classic cars and a working display of antique engines, Owls Head Transportation Museum is one of a small cadre of aviation museums with real flying aircraft. Its exhibitions include special events in the warm months when the engines run and the airplanes fly. According to the curator, Rob Verbsky, "You have to be willing to take on risk with the older planes. It's push pull. To understand a plane you need to see it fly, but if it crashes, history is wiped out. Of our 15 or so aircraft, a number are replicas, with more modern engines."

The location may be off the beaten path, but it is brilliant because of the airfield, the Knox County Regional Airport, next door (two miles from Rockland's business district). The prologue for the museum is an airport built during World War II, in 1944, to train British and U.S. Navy pilots. For the Brits, whose country was a war zone, Owls Head was a safe training locale for novice pilots and possibly less prone to espionage. The U.S. Navy pilots could practice landings and takeoffs from aircraft carriers. The runways had faux carriers for their practices. The endemic fog of the area gave an opportunity to fly in adverse conditions.

Rob Verbsky points to Frank Tallman and Paul Mantz, who bought fleets

Vintage automobile at Owls Head Transportation Museum. *OHTM.*

Biplane at OHTM. *OHTM.*

of planes to film in movies and resold them to private pilots.

The airport had three runways originally for training. In the 1970s, one runway was decommissioned, leaving an unoccupied expanse near Route 73 in the woods. The creation story features Tom Watson Jr., the CEO of IBM, who summered in North Haven and had been a pilot during World War II. Verbsky said:

> *Watson, who transformed IBM from producing punch card computers to digital computers, was in his free time looking to the past. Another airplane buff was Jim Rockefeller Jr., who also had a home, with a runway, in the area. Tom had the idea for a museum while at the graduation of one of his children. He flew to Jim's runway a few weeks later for a chat. They hooked up with Steve Lang, more from the boating side, who knew the local people. An educational space appealed to the community, so Watson and Rockefeller corralled interest to acquire land around the runway. Since the 1970s, the museum has grown in stages. Now, including devices, books and ephemera, it has ten thousand items. People assume that such a collection has to be in a big urban area, but in an urban area, we could not do what we do and show off planes. Because of low traffic, the old vehicles can be taken out for rides, and there are rallies of the owners of antique airplanes and autos, motorcycles and bicycles.*

The museum has an original Curtiss JN-4D, better known as the Curtiss Jenny, the design that made flying more accessible. It was built by the St. Louis Airplane Co. in 1917 and was last used by the U.S. Army Signal Corps in Georgia. The Jennys were built as trainers during World War I, and by the 1920s, most American pilots had learned to fly in them. After World War I, five hundred Jennys were sold, including one to Charles Lindbergh for $500. These were the barnstormers that landed in fields. For many in rural parts like Maine, they proved that flight was real—people saw or got up in Jennys. Now the museum has an original, one of the fewer than six in the world that still fly. It has a replica of the Red Baron's Fokker triplane. You can see the glamorous Cadillacs and Rolls-Royces, the highly decorated Romani vardo wagon or the Cretors popcorn car.

The automobiles represent many ingenious inventions but also stories. The museum has a 1913 Rolls purchased by Alice Longfellow, daughter of the poet Henry Wadsworth Longfellow. She was traveling in style, driven by her chauffeur in a Pierce-Arrow around Europe, when she decided she preferred a 40/50 Silver Ghost Rolls-Royce. She had the car in France at the start of World War I but left Europe for the United States in August 1914; after some repairs and the changes she requested, the Silver Ghost was shipped to her later in the year. Alice Longfellow sold it to Alan Bemis, an MIT professor who did weather research. Professor Bemis used the behemoth to take sensitive equipment up Mount Washington.

Chapter 23
The Wyeths

The light and the colors of St. George, the land and sea, fog, flowers and trees and the ever-changing tide have a special attraction for artists. However, Maine artists are distinguished by low visibility and desire for privacy. They seem happy in relative isolation. For its very non-tourism, St. George was a second home to both N.C. and Andrew Wyeth and has been the primary abode of the famous painter Jamie Wyeth for many years.

The genius of the Wyeths made them America's "First Family of American Art." Actually, they are the second First Family, as there were the Peales of colonial Philadelphia, who held that status before them. Andrew Wyeth, who met his future wife, Betsy, in Cushing, Maine, proposed to her when she was seventeen and he was but a few years older. Andy and Betsy were summer residents of Cushing from the time they were married (1940) until around 1992, when Betsy moved their primary residence to Benner Island full time. They bought Southern Island, across from Tenants Harbor, in the 1970s and maintained the Cushing home. They hopped to Benner Island, but Betsy loved island living more than Andy did.

N.C. Wyeth lived at 8 Bells in Port Clyde until his death, and then Andy Wyeth took over his studio about the time they bought Benner. Andy came ashore from Benner daily and painted at 8 Bells until his death. He commuted from Port Clyde, sailing over to Horse Point Lane in Port Clyde, where he used the house and studio that had been N.C.'s. Meanwhile, their son Jamie Wyeth and his wife were summer residents of St. George for years. (Andy and Betsy never lived on Southern; their primary residence was Cushing the whole time they owned it.) Jamie became the proprietor of Southern Island, where he lives at present, with his own white lighthouse. He spends most of his time there but maintains his farm in Pennsylvania. The hopscotch began when the artist N.C. Wyeth, the inimitable illustrator of pirates and Pilgrims of classic children's books, brought his family to Maine during the summers from Chadds Ford, Pennsylvania.

Jamie was home-schooled after sixth grade, and Andrew gave Jamie half his studio to work in. Andrew played classical music loud when he worked, and Jamie, who prefers working in silence, had the record player in his part of the studio, so he had to paint wearing wax earplugs.

Many local people know Jamie by name or at least sight, as they did Andrew (nicknamed "Uncle Andy"). But they respect Jamie as a person and are grateful for the inobtrusive means by which he and Phyllis, his late wife, contributed to life on the peninsula. Phyllis was a horsewoman until her spine was broken in an automobile accident and she was confined to a wheelchair. Their marriage was a romance that reflected outward to do good—for instance, founding the Herring Gut Learning Center (Factory Road, Port Clyde) to educate local children in their natural world. They led reserved lives, first at Monhegan Island; however, Jamie didn't like having people look over his back, so he began to work inside a cardboard box to eliminate the problem. Then they moved to Southern Island and lived quiet, generous lives. Their foundation, for instance, gave funds to the effort to resurface the Tenants Harbor tennis courts.

Art curator and radio host Irene Rawlings for the *Saturday Evening Post* put it well in saying that Jamie Wyeth "was born in 1946 with a silver paintbrush in his mouth." He is a realist, painting in different styles and also using media in an unorthodox fashion. His father and grandfather were against the tide of fashion for the abstract. "I put paint in my mouth, on my fingers, on toothpicks, and often paint with the wrong end of the brush," Jamie said in the *Saturday Evening Post* interview. He is the epitome of an artist for whom everything is art and every creation is a fresh experience. "His hands are covered with paint, and he revels in painting," a friend of his told me.

A fishing schooner captain said to me, "One day I got a call from Jamie, 'My new boat has gone pooch,' he said. 'Who's got the white boat next to me? I need a tow.' 'Everybody's got a white boat," I told him. 'I'll be right down.'" The artist painted him a picture to say thanks.

Linda Bean, heir to the L.L. Bean fortune, has made two forays in Port Clyde that signal the Wyeths' art. Her gallery at the dock sells prints and

Jamie Wyeth's vessel *Dreadnought* in dock at the Tenants Harbor Boatyard. *Nasser K.*

reproductions, and on Horse Point Lane is the N.C. Wyeth Reading Room, containing materials illustrated by N.C. for research. The Wyeth Center of Art, featuring works by N.C. Wyeth, Andrew Wyeth and Jamie Wyeth, was built in 2010 with funds from the credit card company MBNA and became a striking addition to the Farnsworth Museum.

Jamie Wyeth has a shiny black yacht at the Tenants Harbor Boatyard (impressing boaters for having the luxury of showers). But he doesn't use his large boat to go back and forth to Southern Island. For that, he rows or takes a small powerboat.

Chapter 24

Russell W. Porter

Mainers speak when they have something to say, and given the life in Maine, they have time to finish a sentence! Life does slow down; the sun sets before four o'clock in the afternoon, and ice mottled with mud is so thick that a person considers crawling on all fours to the wood pile. In the longest season, winter, many people shift into their sideline, turning to whatever is their artistry of individual endeavor. The adage "Build a better mousetrap" is attributed to a northern New Englander, Ralph Waldo Emerson, and the picture of people beating a path to your door suggests someone who has been spending a good deal of time alone.

Having earned his bachelor's in architecture at Massachusetts Institute of Technology, Russell Porter followed his passions of exploration and astronomy. He was on an expedition to climb Mount McKinley and then was the first assistant scientist on the Baldwin-Ziegler expedition to the North Pole, both exciting adventures, although neither reached its goal. While he was stuck in the ice for three seasons in the Arctic expedition since the sailing vessel that was supposed to pick up the forty men sank, he studied the stars, made maps and painted pictures of his encampment and portraits of Inuks he got to know.

Then he was ready to settle down—perhaps to start an art colony and tinker with a design for a telescope. Natural to Porter, he consulted maps and, without having been there, chose Port Clyde as the location on the coast, as it had an exceptionally clear night sky.

Russell W. Porter's observatory was located where he lived at Land's End, Port Clyde. *Aidan Kaczynski.*

Restoring the abandoned 1820s Marshall family farm and studying the stars would occupy the young bachelor, but he was a little lonely. Berton C. Willard, his biographer, tells the story of how the first time Porter walked down to the center of the village, he went into the post office and met his future wife. Alfred Marshall was a fisherman and the town clerk who had sold Porter the house on the point. The young lady at the window was Marshall's daughter Alice Belle. A first-class stamp was two cents, and Porter politely stated that he needed two stamps to Boston. "That will be four cents in all," the young lady told him, adding, "You're new in town?" Being slightly deaf, he had to ask her to repeat this. Thus, their courtship commenced. Through her mother, Alice Belle Marshall was the fifth great-granddaughter of the patriarch of Marshall Point Lighthouse, Samuel Marshall Sr., and through her father the third great-granddaughter.

Russell and Alice married in 1907. The couple announced they would honeymoon in Rockland (an indication of how slow travel was), but they stealthily turned the horse and buggy back to spend their wedding night in their own home. Porter eventually became a professor of architecture at MIT and returned with his wife and daughter to Port Clyde each summer and for many holidays, but first he tried to make a living in the village, initially raising potatoes and then surveying and building cottages at Land's End, with a friend, to rent. Each of the fourteen cottages was of a different design. Several remain off the point between the Marshall Point Lighthouse and Drift Inn Beach, off Cottage Road. Tall stone pillars that Porter erected and inscribed "1906" can be seen on either side of the main road. Using stone from the walls that crisscrossed the area of Land's End, he built a guest house he called the Castle, also extant.

Figuring it out as you go along is a proud character of Mainers, so Russell fit right in. For his development of the two-hundred-inch Hale Telescope, he is considered the founder of American amateur astronomy. He valued the development of the telescope most of his accomplishments, writing to a friend happily in 1946, "I have helped towards giving thousands of people the pleasure of creating with their own hands a tool to unlock the wonders of the heavens."

Bibliography

Rockland

Barron, Gene, and Andrew Carpenter. *The Clipper Ships of Rockland, Maine.* Thomaston: Maine Authors Publishing, 2017.

Barry, William David. *Maine: The Wilder Half of New England.* Gardiner, ME: Tilbury House, 2012.

Bench, Raney. "Maine's Gone Mad: The Rising of the Klan." Main History Documents, 224. 2019. digitalcommons.library.umaine.edu/mainehistory/224.

Bird, John. *Rockland: Rise and Renewal.* Rockland, ME: Rockland Historical Society, 2019.

Botstein, Leon. "American Harmonies: The Music of Walter Piston." Performed March 29, 2011, at Carnegie Hall, New York, New York, by the American Symphony Orchestra. Americansymphony.org.

Brooks, Noah. *Henry Knox: A Soldier of the Revolution.* Cranbury, NJ: Scholar's Bookshelf, 2005.

Caldwell, Bill. *Enjoying Maine.* Portland, ME: Guy Gannett, 1977.

Dietz, Lew, et al. *A Special Place: A History of Oyster River Bog.* Rockland, ME: Rockport Conservation Commission, 1976.

Donnelly, Tim. "The Delicious History of the American Donut." *New York Post,* June 6, 2014. nypost.com/2014/06/06/the-delicious-history-of-the-American-donut.

Fagan, William Francis. "From Lime Kilns to Art Galleries: A Historical Anthropogeography of the Maine Coast City of Rockland." PhD diss., Louisiana State University, 2003. digital commons.lsu.edu/gradschool_dissertations/208.

Forbes-Robertson, Diana. *My Aunt Maxine: The Story of Maxine Elliott.* New York: Viking, 1964.

Gould, Edward K. *Major-General Hiram G. Berry, His Career as Contractor, Bank President, Politician and Major-General of Volunteers in the Civil War.* Rockland, ME: Press of the Courier-Gazette, 1899.

Harden, Brian R., ed. *Shore Village Story: An Informal History of Rockland, Maine.* Rockland, ME: Courier-Gazette, Inc., 1989.

Hardy, Kerry. *Notes on a Lost Flute: A Field Guide to the Wabanaki.* Camden, ME: Down East, 2009.

Hopkins, Stephen D. *Red Jacket: The Life and Times of a Maine Clipper Ship.* Rockland, ME: Rockland Historical Society, 2016.

Johnson, Charles W. *Bogs of the Northeast.* Hanover, NH: University Press of New England, 1985.

Judd, Richard. "Canoes, Schooners and the Down-Easter." Maine History Online. www.mainememory.net/sitebuilder/site/831/page1241.

Komanecky, Michael K. "The Merchant's Tale." *The Magazine Antiques*, July–August 2014, 130–37.

Linder, Mark. "Mumford's Metaphors: Sticks and Stones versus Ships and the Sea." *Journal of Architectural Education* 46, no. 2 (November 1992): 95–103. www.jstor.org/stable/1425203.

Lisle, Laurie. *Louise Nevelson: A Passionate Life.* New York: Summit Books.

Maine, Government of. Focus Areas of Statewide Ecological Significance. Rockland Bog. www.maine.gov/dacf/mnap/focusarea/rockland_bog_focus_area.pdf.

Maine Preservation. *Ask an Old House Pro. Reading Historic Roofs* (Maine Homes by DownEast, January 31, 2018).

Mauck, Bjorn, Nele Glaser, Wolfhard Schlosser and Guido Dehnhardt. "Harbor Seals (*Phoca vitulina*) Can Steer by the Stars." *Animal Cognition* 11 (May 2008): 715–18.

Meroz, Y. "Calligan's Los Rongorongo, and Some Shipwrecks." *Rapa Nui Journal: Journal of the Easter Island Foundation* 17, no. 8 (October 2003). kahualike.manoa.hawaii.edu/rnj/vol17/issa/8.

Milford, Nancy. *Savage Beauty: The Life of Edna St. Vincent Millay.* New York: Random House, 2001.

Miller, Dorcas. *The Maine Coast: A Nature Lover's Guide.* N.p.: East Woods Press in cooperation with the Maine Audubon Society, 1979.

Moores, Lawrence Wayne, Jr. "The History of the Ku Klux Klan in Maine, 1922–1931." Master's thesis, University of Maine, 1950. digitalcommons.library.umaine.edu/etd/3239.

Morey, David C. *The Voyage of* Archangell*: James Rosier's Account of the Weymouth Voyage of 1605: A True Relation.* Thomaston, ME: Tilbury House, 2005.

Morison, Samuel Eliot. *The Story of Mt. Desert, Maine.* Boston: Little, Brown, 1960.

Morris, Ann. *A History of Blackington's Corner and the Highlands: 200 Years of Farms and Quarries.* Rockland, ME: Rockland Historical Society.

———. *A Walk along Main Street.* Rockland, ME: Lake Avenue Publishing Co., 2015.

Nash, Steven E. *Reconstruction's Ragged Edge: The Politics of Postwar Life in the Southern Mountains.* Chapel Hill: University of North Carolina Press, 2016.

National Park Service. "Tales of a Silver Ghost: Alice Longfellow's Rolls Royce." www.nps.gov/articles/tales-of-a-silver-ghost-alice-longfelllows-rolls-royce.htm.

New England Historical Society. "Mary Patten, 19 and Pregnant, Takes Command of a Clipper Ship in 1856." www.newenglandhistoricalsociety.com/mary-patten-19-pregnant-commands-clipper-ship-1856.

Nunes, Jadviga da Costa. "Red Jacket: The Man and His Portraits." *American Art Journal* 12, no. 3 (Summer 1980): 4–20. www.jstor.org/stable/1594231.

Pulls, Mark. *Henry Knox, Visionary General of the American Revolution.* London: Palgrave Macmillan, 2008.

Rockland Courier-Gazette. "Invention of the Lobster Roll, 1927, Rockland, ME." December 22, 1953.

Shore Village Historical Society. *Around Rockland*: *Images of America.* Mount Pleasant, SC: Arcadia Publishing, 1996.

Smith, Richard Oliver. "Architecture and Boat Building: Connecting with Spolia." Master's thesis, Azieli School of Architecture and Urbanism, Carlton University, Ottawa, Ontario, 2009. Library and Archives Canada, Ottawa.

Washington Post. "'Old Salt' Doughnut Hole Inventor Tells Just How Discovery Was Made and Stomachs of Earth Saved." March 26, 1916, ES9.

Weber, Jill E., Sally C. Rooney and Jennifer Atkinson, eds. "Natural and Cultural Resource of the Oyster River Bog." Oyster River Bog Association, 2002.

Whitehead, Ruth Holmes. *The Old Man Told Us: Excerpts from Micmac History, 1500–1950.* Halifax, Nova Scotia: Nimbus, 1991.

Williams, Paul K., and Kelton C. Higgins. *Cleveland Park.* Mount Pleasant, SC: Arcadia Publishing, 2003.

Woodard, Colin. *The Lobster Coast: Rebels, Rusticators, and the Struggle for a Forgotten Frontier.* New York: Penguin, 2004.

Woollcott, Alexander. "The Truth about Jessica Dermott." In *While Rome Burns.* New York: Viking, 1934.

Zerby, Nancy. "Name That House! A Guide to New England Architectural Style for the Roadside Historian." *New England Today*. newengland.com/today/living/homes/new-england-architecture.

St. George

Andriote, John-Manuel. "The History, Science and Poetry of New England's Stone Walls." *Earth: The Sciences behind the Headlines*, May 13, 2014. www.earthmagazine.org/article/history-science-and-poetry-new-englands-stone-walls.

Balano, James W. *The Log of the Skipper's Wife.* Camden, ME: Down East Books, 1979.

Barry, William David. *Maine: The Wilder Half of New England.* Gardiner, ME: Tilbury House, 2012.

Blanchard, Paula. *Sarah Orne Jewett: Her World and Her Work.* New York: Delacorte, 1994.

Duncan, Robert E. *Coastal Maine: A Maritime History.* New York: W.W. Norton, 1992.

Kistler, Linda H., Clairmont P. Carter and Brackston Hinchey. "Planning and Control in the 19th Century Ice Trade." *Accounting Historians Journal* 11, no. 1 (Spring 1984): 19–30.

Morey, David C. *The Voyage of* Archangell: *James Rosier's Account of the Weymouth Voyage of 1605: A True Relation.* Thomaston, ME: Tilbury House, 2005.

Picard, Dennis D. *Harvesting Ice in New England, 1926–1957.* Bucksport, ME: Northeast Historical Films, 2017.

Platt, David, ed. *One Land/Two Worlds: A Symposium to Celebrate the 400th Anniversary of George Weymouth's Voyage to New England.* Rockland, ME: Island Institute, 2005.

Resource Inventory of the Georges River Land Trust, Maine. Submitted January 1989, conducted by QLF/Atlantic Center for the Environment.

Silverthorne, Elizabeth. *Sarah Orne Jewett: A Writer's Life.* Woodstock, NY: Overlook Press, 1993.

Skoglund, James. *First Baptist Church of St. George, Maine, 1789–1989.* N.p., n.d.

Smalley, Albert J. *History of St. George, Maine.* Typescript, 1969.

Snow, Edward Rowe. *The Lighthouses of New England.* Beverly, MA: Commonwealth Editions, an imprint of Memoirs, 2002.

St. George Comprehensive Plan Committee. *St. George Comprehensive Plan*, May 2018.

St. George Historical Society. stgeorgehistory.com.

Sullivan, Steven E., and Robert L. Welsch. *Cemetery Inscriptions and Burial Sites of St. George, Maine and the Nearby Islands.* Rockland, ME: Penobscot Press, 2009.

Willard, Berton C. *Russell O. Porter: Arctic Explorer, Artist, Telescope Maker.* Freeport, ME: Bond Wheelwright Co., 1976.

Willey, Tammy L. *The St. George Peninsula.* Mount Pleasant, SC: Arcadia Publishing, 2005.

About the Author

Because New York City was the place for a freelance writer to live, Jane Merrill began her career there. Now she lives in St. George and summers on the Bay of Fundy. Her branch of the Merrills were Maine forest clearers. Some left for the West after the Eric Canal was built and later returned. Her great-grandmother was a musical theater performer on Peak's Island, the family home. She is the author of many books, her favorites being about Aaron Burr's escapades in Paris, the iconic Parisian showgirl costume, the inventor-diplomat Sir Benjamin Thompson and the afterlife of Benedict Arnold.